The "Twenty-

A Regimental H

Winthrop Dudley Sheldon

Alpha Editions

This edition published in 2024

ISBN : 9789362515339

Design and Setting By
Alpha Editions
www.alphaedis.com
Email - info@alphaedis.com

As per information held with us this book is in Public Domain.
This book is a reproduction of an important historical work. Alpha Editions uses the best technology to reproduce historical work in the same manner it was first published to preserve its original nature. Any marks or number seen are left intentionally to preserve its true form.

CHAPTER I.
CAMP NEAR WASHINGTON.

"As by the west wind driven, the ocean waves
Dash forward on the far-resounding shore,
Wave upon wave: first curls the ruffled sea,
With whit'ning crests; anon with thundering roar
It breaks upon the beach, and, from the crags
Recoiling, flings in giant curves its head
Aloft, and tosses high the wild sea-spray,
Column on column—so the hosts of Greece
Poured ceaseless to the war."

HOMER.

The campaign of the Twenty-seventh Regiment Connecticut Volunteers began in the most critical and anxious period of the war against the rebellion—the year 1862. After long months of diligent preparation, the Army of the Potomac opened the year with its first memorable advance against the rebel capital. The inspiring faith of all loyal hearts followed every step of its progress up the Peninsula, toward the stronghold of treason; and when the shattered but undaunted remnants retreated down the James river, and hurried to the defence of the national capital, menaced by an exultant foe, deep was the disappointment which filled the whole North. Every ear was strained to catch the result of the conflict before Washington, only to hear that the rebels had been partially successful, and were crossing the Potomac into Maryland and Pennsylvania. Those were days of profound anxiety, but not of weak irresolution. Each new disaster seemed to bring the people nearer to a realization of the magnitude of the struggle, and nerve them to fulfil the imperative duties of the hour. The President, early in July, issued his Proclamation, calling for three hundred thousand men, to serve for three years; and on the fourth of August following summoned to the field three hundred thousand more, to serve for nine months. The Twenty-seventh Regiment was organized under this latter call. Its members were recruited from New-Haven county, and mainly from the city of New-Haven, with considerable numbers from Madison, Milford, Meriden, Wallingford, Branford, Clinton, and Guilford, and still smaller quotas from other neighboring towns.

The character and material of the regiment well illustrated the heartiness with which all classes responded to the earnest call of the President in those dark days of the Republic. Every variety of condition and employment found representatives in the Twenty-seventh. The agricultural population of the county responded with a goodly number of the votaries of Ceres. Many of the most respected and enterprising mechanics and business men of the community laid aside for a season the implements of their labor to join its ranks. Members of the press exchanged pen and type for sword and bayonet. There were also several accomplished engineers in the regiment, one of whom was detailed in that department, on the staff of General W. S. Hancock, and had charge of the General's topographical maps and plans of battles. The public schools of the city contributed one of their most esteemed teachers, who gave his life on the field of Fredericksburg; and in the room where of yore he so successfully led on his pupils from step to step in knowledge, hangs his portrait, to them a daily-recurring lesson of noble patriotism and self-devotion. Also the various professions furnished of their members; and old Yale, never faithless to the patriotic instincts of her Revolutionary sons, was represented by several of her graduates and students, one of whom was a color-bearer of the regiment at Fredericksburg, Chancellorsville, and Gettysburg.

The first company went into camp at Camp Terry, New-Haven, in the latter part of August, and by the middle of September the whole number of companies were on the ground, with nearly a full quota of men. Being technically a militia regiment, the choice of field officers was vested in those of the line. Richard S. Bostwick, of New-Haven, was elected Colonel; Henry C. Merwin, of the same place, Lieutenant-Colonel; and Theodore Byxbee, of Meriden, Major; all of whom, with a number of the company officers, had been connected with the three-months volunteers at the beginning of the war. After several weeks spent in perfecting the organization and equipment, the regiment was mustered into the United States service, October twenty-second, 1862, for the term of nine months, and started for the field in the evening of that day, numbering eight hundred and twenty-nine, rank and file.

Without stopping to dwell upon the passage to New-York, to Port Monmouth, or upon the generous hospitality of the Quaker City, and passing by the night journey to Baltimore, succeeded by a day's rest on the pavements of that city, the morning of the twenty-fifth found us in Washington. Camp Seward, on Arlington Heights, is soon reached, and quickly long rows of tents rear their white roofs in General Lee's peach orchard. Possibly in other days we should have been summarily ejected by a grand charge of that gentleman's dusky retainers, or perhaps indicted in the courts for presuming to trespass upon the domain of an F. F. V., and have paid dearly to appease his injured feelings. But now the crowd of slaves is dispersed, and "Massa Lee" is not there to dispute our right to possession.

Our introduction to the Old Dominion would be incomplete unless the foreground of the picture presented to view that bugbear, Virginia mud, which has made and unmade so many Generals, and stopped the wheels of the Army of the Potomac with periodical regularity. We had hardly arrived at Camp Seward when the clouds began to marshal their forces for an illustration of their power to change the sacred soil into a sea of mud; and as if to show the minutiæ of the forming process, it began to drizzle slowly; the mist gradually enlarged into drops, and the soil grew softer and softer. As we floundered about, we began to realize that the aforesaid mud was not altogether a myth, conjured up by inefficient commanders to excuse inaction. The storm continued at intervals during the twenty-sixth, and, as night approached, a strong wind, superadded to the pelting rain, swept howling over the ridge, tearing many of our tents from their uncertain moorings. All, however, were disposed to view philosophically this somewhat unceremonious welcome to the soil of Virginia, and the hardships of a soldier's life.

At noon of the twenty-seventh the order came to strike tents, preparatory to moving our camp a few miles up the Potomac. Late in the day the march began. Crossing over into Georgetown, by the Aqueduct Bridge, and following the picturesque course of the river up to Chain Bridge, we return to the left bank, and bivouack for the rest of the night around huge fires. The next morning Camp Tuttle assumes a veritable existence, and here the Twenty-seventh settle down to a month's routine and drill, preliminary to the rough experience of an actual campaign. Our camp was situated upon a rising ground, from which could be seen the majestic dome of the Capitol. Some distance in front of the parade, and on the left, were thick woods, while the right was skirted by a road, across which were encamped the Twenty-fourth and Twenty-eighth New-Jersey, and the One Hundred and Twenty-seventh Pennsylvania, which, with our own regiment, constituted a brigade of Abercrombie's division of the army, for the defence of Washington. As soon as the camp was established in its new location, the Colonel issued a regimental order, setting forth the programme of daily duty as follows: Reveille at six A.M.; guard mounting at eight; company drill from nine to eleven, and again from one to two; battalion drill from three to four, and dress parade at five P.M.; tattoo at nine, taps at half-past nine. All this was varied by an occasional season of picket duty, a few miles up the Leesburg turnpike.

Our first Sabbath at Camp Tuttle forms, in most respects, a sample of all the rest. Sunday is to the soldier the most anomalous day of the calendar, especially if situated, as we were, without a chaplain. The weekly inspection and freedom from drill are the chief points which distinguish it from other days. In the present instance, however, an unexpected cause of excitement appeared. After dress parade, it was announced that in consequence of certain rumored movements of the enemy in the direction of Leesburg, it might be necessary to beat the long roll, to call the regiment under arms at any moment during the night. Of course, the very thought of a rebel added new zest to our military existence. Every one was on the *qui vive*, and made his arrangements to respond to the call with the utmost promptness. But the apprehended raid did not take place, and our rest was therefore undisturbed by the soul-stirring notes of the long roll.

Every few days a company was detailed to go on picket—an event not altogether unwelcome, as a relief to the monotonous round of camp duties, and as an introduction to a new phase of experience. To obtain some idea of this portion of our regimental life around Washington, let us "fall in," fully armed and equipped, and follow one of these parties to the picket-line. On the present occasion, Company H, with detachments from other regiments, started out one morning, and, after marching several miles on the Leesburg Turnpike, arrived about ten o'clock at the village of Langley. The line of pickets extended along the main road a short distance beyond the centre of the place, and also along a cross-road, which, coming up from the south, connects with the turnpike just before we reach the village. Houses, favorably situated at different points, were occupied as headquarters of the various squads, or, if such conveniences were not at hand, brush huts supplied their place. At that time Langley consisted of about a dozen houses, and one small church, and had once been favored with two regular taverns, whose sphere was now filled by two boarding-houses of minor importance, one of which indicated its character to the public by the sign:

	RESTER
	ANT

The dinner hour having arrived, the pickets unanimously conclude to set aside Uncle Sam's homely fare, and take advantage of the enlarged facilities of entertainment afforded by the village. Accordingly they adjourn to one of the boarding-houses, kept by a man of secession proclivities, whose principles, however, do not interfere with his untiring efforts to please. Such houses of refreshment, where a civilized meal could be obtained, situated as they were here and there along the picket-line, added much to the enjoyment of these brief excursions from camp. Our duties were not very onerous, requiring the attention of each man two hours out of every six, and consisted in seeing that no one passed along the road, or appeared in the vicinity, without proper authority. In good weather, the two days of picket duty, occurring once a fortnight, were quite agreeable; but if stormy, they afforded good material for the grumbling fraternity.

In view of the approach of winter, and the probability of remaining in our present location for some time, it was thought best to make corresponding preparations. Pine logs, with considerable labor, were cut and brought in from the neighboring forest, and soon Camp Tuttle began to present an air of comfort positively inviting. But after only a brief enjoyment of our improved quarters, and as if to remind us of the uncertainty always attending the soldier's life, orders came, November eighteenth, for Company H to strike tents, pack up, and march over to Hall's Hill, there to clear up a place for the regimental encampment. Arriving on the hill in a pelting rain, huge fires were built of the brush and stumps which covered the ground, and by evening our tents were up, and we were as comfortable as circumstances would allow. Hearing of several deserted encampments about a mile distant, on Miner's and Upton's Hills, many parties went out the next morning to secure anything which might add to their convenience. A large barren plain was covered far and wide with the huts and *débris* of a portion of McClellan's army, which encamped here in the winter of 1862. The whole presented a very curious and suggestive sight. Meanwhile, orders came to strike tents and rejoin the regiment. It appeared that all the regiments in the vicinity were ordered to prepare for a rapid march. The Army of the Potomac had but recently crossed the river, after the battle of Antietam, in pursuit of Lee, and the enemy were said to be threatening General Sigel, in command at Centreville. In view of this state of affairs, the reserve, in the defences of Washington, was called upon to be ready for any emergency. Returning to camp, we found the men earnestly canvassing the nature of the contemplated march. The orders, however, were countermanded in the evening, perhaps in consequence of a severe storm, which continued for several days.

CHAPTER II.
TO THE FRONT.

The soldier who is untried in the fearful ordeal of war looks forward with a kind of adventurous excitement to the time when he shall cross swords with the enemy; and especially if his heart is bound up in the cause, and his motives lie deeper than mere love of adventure, he desires to stand at the post of duty, though it be in the deadly charge, and at the cannon's mouth.

At length the last day of November, a beautiful Sabbath, came, and with it marching orders. All attention was now concentrated upon the movement to take place the next day, at nine o'clock. The cooks were busy preparing rations for the march; the men were arranging their traps in the most portable form, and all looked forward with eager interest to the new scenes before us. At the appointed time, on the following morning, the Twenty-seventh, with the other regiments in the brigade, began the march for Washington, leaving our comparatively commodious A tents standing. Henceforth, shelter-tents, and for much of the time no tents at all, were to be our covering. Our final destination was all a mystery, until, as the days advanced, conjecture was enabled, with some probability, to fix upon Fredericksburg. The march across Chain Bridge, through Georgetown and Washington, and down the Potomac, fifteen miles, consumed the first day, and that night a tired set slept beneath their shelter-tents, nestling in the woods by the road-side.

By eight o'clock, December second, we were again in motion, and before sundown accomplished the appointed distance of twenty miles, through a pleasant country, divided into large and apparently well-cultivated plantations. Sambo's glittering ivory and staring eyes gleamed from many gateways, greeting us half suspiciously. One young colored boy concluded he had been beaten quite long enough by his master, and not liking the prospect before him if he remained in slavery, thought best to join the column, and march to freedom. In anticipation of some such proceedings on the part of the colored population, the planters of that region patrolled the roads on horseback, watching our ranks as we filed past, to see if some luckless contraband were not harbored therein.

The third day brought us within three miles of Port Tobacco, and without standing on ceremony, we encamped for the night on the grounds of a secessionist planter, and availed ourselves of his abundant store of hay and straw. December fourth, we passed through the town—a very ordinary, shabby-looking place, whose secession population hardly designed to glance at us, except from behind closed shutters.

Thus far the weather had been delightful, but the fifth day of our march, and the last on the Maryland side of the Potomac, opened rather inauspiciously, and by the time we reached the river bank at Liverpool Point, a cold rainstorm had set in, in which we were obliged to stand a couple of hours awaiting our turn to be ferried across to Acquia Landing. At length the rain changed into driving snow, and when we arrived at the Landing, the surrounding hills were white with the generous deposit. The village at Acquia Creek, after being evacuated sundry times, had risen again from the ashes of several burnings to become the base of supplies for Burnside's army before Fredericksburg. Busy carpenters were rearing storehouses, eventually to take their turn at conflagration, and the offing was full of vessels of every description, loaded with stores to be transferred by rail to Falmouth.

In the snow we disembarked, and after many delays reached our camping ground, on a hill-side, a mile or more up the railroad. It was now evening, and the prospect seemed anything but encouraging, in view of the fact that the storm continued with even augmented fury. We pitched our shelter-tents and made our beds in the snow, and built fires, under difficulties which can hardly be exaggerated. To add to the discomfort of the case, our supplies were entirely exhausted, and although the wharves and storehouses at the Landing fairly groaned with pork and hard-tack, we could not obtain these articles, owing to inflexible red tape, and in part to the fact that the railroad was monopolized in carrying subsistence for the army at Falmouth. A very limited supply of sawdust ginger-cakes constituted the universal bill of fare until the evening of the next day.

December sixth dawned upon us, cold and frosty, but clear—just such weather as graces the month in the latitude of New-England. The discomforts of the preceding day were soon forgotten in the cheerful sunshine. At this time our worthy chaplain, Rev. J. W. Leek, joined the regiment. Though separated from us in one short week, by reason of an almost fatal wound, yet in that brief period he had gained the hearty respect and esteem of all, and connected his name most honorably with the history of the Twenty-seventh.

After a rest of two days, we bade adieu to Acquia Creek on the morning of December eighth, and resumed our march to Falmouth. Having lost our way, the journey, which properly required but one day, occupied until noon of the next, when we arrived at the headquarters of General D. N. Couch, at that time in command of the Second Army Corps. By him the Twenty-seventh was assigned to the Third Brigade, General S. K. Zook's, of the First Division, commanded by General W. S. Hancock. At this time the Army of the Potomac was divided into three grand divisions—the right, left, and centre—the first, of which our corps formed a part, under the command of General Edwin V. Sumner.

We were now marched off to our camping ground, a short distance from the Rappahannock river. Henceforth the fortunes of the Twenty-seventh are linked with the Army of the Potomac. The regiment belonged to a corps whose thinned ranks eloquently testified to the hard-fought contests of the Peninsula, where it had borne the brunt, always in the fore-front of battle, and the last to retire when retreat became necessary. The history of the Second proved it to be one of the most reliable corps in the service—always ready for any desperate encounter under its brave and fighting leaders. The famous Irish Brigade formed a part of our division. Such being the character and history of the corps, it was evident that the Twenty-seventh must now make up its mind to the severest of campaign service. Scarcely were our tents up, when the Colonel received orders to have the company cooks prepare four days' rations, to be ready by the next morning—the inevitable preliminary to more important events.

The forenoon of December tenth was occupied in cleaning our arms and preparing for an inspection, to take place at twelve o'clock, before General Zook and staff. Perhaps at this point it might be well to speak of the weapons the General was called upon to inspect, and which he declared unfit for service. One of his staff, a day or two later, remarked: "Boys, if you can't discharge them, you can use the bayonet." That certainly was the most serviceable part of the gun. At the outset, the Twenty-seventh, with the exception of the flank companies, was furnished with Austrian rifles of such an inferior order that no regular inspector would have passed them. Scarcely one of these weapons was without defects in the most essential particulars. These facts are not mentioned to bring discredit upon any of the authorities cognizant of such matters, but simply as a matter of justice to the regiment. Doubtless the best of reasons could have been given to justify the temporary distribution of such arms. Early, however, in the following January, the regiment was supplied with the Whitney rifled musket, a weapon in the highest degree satisfactory to all.

CHAPTER III.
FREDERICKSBURG.

In the afternoon of the tenth, two hundred and fifty men of the Twenty-seventh were detailed to picket along the Rappahannock above Falmouth. During all the following night might be heard an unusual rumbling of cars, bringing up subsistence from Acquia Creek, and the rattling of ammunition wagons and pontoon trains, slowly moving to their respective destinations. At half-past four, on the morning of the eleventh, the Colonel passed around to the officers' quarters, giving orders to have their companies supplied with three days' rations, and fall in by half-past six, in light marching order. Let us leave the scene of busy preparation in camp, and for a few moments view the events transpiring on the river. Three points had been carefully selected by General Burnside where bridges were to be thrown across—one a short distance above the Lacey House, another a few rods below the railroad bridge, and the third about two miles below the city. Boat after boat is anchored in its place; plank after plank is laid in quick succession, and the river is well-nigh spanned by the trembling structure, when suddenly two signal guns break on the still night air, and a sheet of flame bursts from houses on the opposite bank, where hundreds of sharp-shooters lie concealed. The defenceless bridge builders are temporarily driven from their work, while the cannon from the bluffs behind belch forth a defiant response to the rebel challenge.

To return to the Twenty-seventh. Promptly at half-past six the regiment fell in and joined the rest of the brigade, a short distance from camp. Silently, through woods and across fields, we marched to the corps rendezvous, in a deep hollow near the Phillips House, where General Sumner had his headquarters. On the way we passed long lines of troops moving rapidly to the river, or resting behind rows of musket stacks. Here we were to remain until a crossing could be effected.

Meanwhile, the frequency of cannon discharges increases. Every moment another adds its voice to the swelling volume, until from twenty batteries, comprising more than a hundred guns, arranged along the banks of the river, bursts a tempest of shot and shell over the rebel city. This continues, with little cessation, until noon. For three hours following, only occasionally a gun disturbs the comparative quiet. Then the ball opens again with renewed violence. A visit to the top of the hill, overlooking the city, reveals columns of smoke, with now and then a flash of flame, testifying to the effectiveness of the bombardment. At the river, all attempts to complete the pontoon bridge had hitherto failed.

With particular interest we gazed upon a regiment of the corps, as, tired, dusty, and powder smeared, it rejoined us after a protracted effort at the bridge. History records but few parallels to the more than heroic valor which crowned that day's work. A trusty weapon supports the soldier's courage, but to stand, unarmed, the target of unerring sharp-shooters, unable to respond to their attacks, and in view of almost inevitable death, is the highest test of courage. It became evident that the bridge could be completed only by driving the sharp-shooters from the houses on the opposite side, by a sudden dash across the river. This hazardous duty was intrusted to the Seventh Michigan and detachments from several other regiments, and nobly was it performed. The rebels were driven from their hiding-places, the bridge touched the opposite shore, and the first act in this fearful drama closed. This success was received with universal joy, and all attention now concentrated in what the future should unfold. General Howard's division of the Second Corps crossed over into the city, while Hancock's and French's bivouacked for the night in a strip of woods near the Phillips House.

Early the next morning, December twelfth, we crossed into Fredericksburg, over the bridge which had cost so much blood and labor the preceding day. Evidences of the bombardment everywhere presented themselves, in the houses perforated with shot and shell, and in the miscellaneous rubbish which hindered our progress through the street. Mattresses, pitchers, chairs, kitchen utensils, and other furniture, scattered about in grotesque confusion, testified that those who had passed the night in the town had availed themselves of all the comforts within reach. We moved down Water street, and halted at the first pontoon bridge, a few rods below the railroad, where we encamped that day and night. The Twenty-seventh spent the day in bridging gullies and mud-holes with boards and planks from neighboring fences, so that the artillery could pass. Company B was detailed to lay pontoons across a stream uniting with the Rappahannock just below the town. About the middle of the afternoon the rebel batteries attempted to annoy the men engaged in these preparations, and for a time a very brisk artillery duel was maintained between the opposing forces. Sheltered as we were by the steep bank, the rebels could not obtain accurate range, and most of the shells shrieked harmlessly over our heads, and fell into the river or struck on the opposite side.

At length the eventful thirteenth arrived—a day full of scenes and experiences which will never fade from the memory of those who participated in them. Immediately after breakfast we were marched up to Caroline street, the principal street of the town, parallel with the river. Here the division was formed in line of battle, and stacked arms, while arrangements were being completed to storm the heights back of the city.

Staff officers were riding in hot haste to and fro, carrying orders, or disposing the forces, and occasionally our division general, Hancock, rode slowly and proudly up and down the line, surveying the ranks, his countenance wearing an aspect of quiet and cool determination. At length the sound of cannonading comes to our ears from below, indicating that General Franklin has entered upon the task assigned him, of seizing the railroad and turning the enemy's flank. Like banks of keys in a great organ, the rebel works rise behind the town, and gradually the chorus of notes bursts forth directly in front of us. The rebel shell crash among the houses or strike in the street, while the batteries of the Second Corps, on the north bank of the Rappahannock, send their shrieking replies over the city. "Attention!" rings out loud and long above the din. Every man is in his place, his musket at a shoulder. "Right face!" "Right shoulder shift arms!" follow in quick succession. At this moment General Hancock rides up to the Twenty-seventh, and leaning forward in his saddle, with his right arm upraised, briefly addresses them: "You are the only Connecticut regiment in my division. Bring no dishonor upon the State you represent." The order is given, "Forward! March!" reëchoed by commanders of brigades, regiments, and companies, and we move in quick time down the street to the railroad.

While the column is moving on, let us briefly survey the position of the battle-field. Fredericksburg is situated in a large amphitheatre, admirably adapted for defence. Directly in the rear of the town is a smooth field with a slightly ascending grade, extending back a little less than half a mile to the telegraph road, which is flanked by a stone wall, beyond which rises a ridge somewhat abruptly from a hundred to a hundred and fifty feet high. This range of high ground extends as far as Hazel Run, a little stream emptying into the Rappahannock just below the lower edge of the town, and in the other direction bends toward the river, which it very nearly touches just above Falmouth, about a mile above Fredericksburg. Rebel batteries were strongly posted along this eminence, so that a front and enfilading fire could be secured upon any force advancing across the level plateau. General Longstreet was in command of these lines of fortifications, while Stonewall Jackson commanded the rebel right, opposite General Franklin, the whole under the supreme direction of General Lee. Bearing in mind that the task before us was to capture these formidable heights, let us return to the storming column.

Sheltered in a measure by the houses, it passes down Caroline street with little interruption; but as soon as we arrived at the railroad dépôt, several rebel guns, trained upon the spot with fatal accuracy, welcome us to the encounter. Very near this point fell Captain Schweizer, the first of the long list of casualties which at nightfall told how fearfully the conflict had decimated the ranks of the Twenty-seventh. Several were knocked down, one of whom, leaping up, exclaimed earnestly, "I'll have pay for that!" then springing to his place, rushed on to death, for no one ever saw or heard of him afterward. The division now advanced at a double-quick into the open field; then, after resting a few moments on the ground, at the order, "Charge!" moved by the left flank with fixed bayonets, passing French's division, which had been obliged to fall back. A second brief rest, then on again, while shot and shell plow the ground in front, burst over our heads, or make fearful gaps in the line. Yet on we rush. The wounded are left where they fall. Not a word is spoken, not a gun fired. As we approach nearer the rebel lines, all the elements of destruction ingenuity can devise or position afford, are concentrated upon the narrow space. From rows of rifle-pits, protected by a heavy stone wall, bursts a continuous roll of musketry; from neighboring houses flashes the deadly fire of sharp-shooters, while batteries posted on the heights behind strong field-works, and supported by infantry, sweep the field with shot and shell and grape and canister. Enfilading batteries on the right and left of the rebel semicircle pour in their swift discharges, and behind us, the batteries of the Second Corps, on the other side of the river, shell the enemy's works with little effect at the distance of nearly three thousand yards, but with so much danger to the storming party, that General Couch orders them to cease firing. The line now begins to waver, and, with some disorder, presses forward to a brick house, from which a brisk musketry fire is kept up in the direction of the stone wall. At this time the various regiments became mingled together, and, unfortunately, at the order to deploy into line to renew the charge, the Twenty-seventh, in consequence of the confusion, separated into several fragments, advancing to the right and left of the house. The time for a sudden dash had passed, and unable longer to stem the avalanche of fire, which seemed to gather intensity as we proceeded, the charge was continued only as far as a board fence, all full of bullet holes and torn with shot, less than a hundred yards from the famous stone wall, as estimated by an officer of the regiment who afterward visited the spot under flag of truce. With the exception of a partially successful attempt to approach still nearer the rebel rifle-pits, the men remained at this point the rest of the afternoon, loading their guns on the ground, then rising sufficiently to deliver their fire.

The rebel musketry continued with almost uninterrupted violence until night overshadowed the scene, never entirely ceasing in our front. At times it surged off to another part of the line, with only a scattering fire opposite our position; then rolled back again with redoubled power, the peculiar rattling of separate discharges being fused into one prolonged sound. Lines of rebel troops could be seen marching along the ridge, and running down to aid their comrades in the rifle-pits below. But for a weary two hours no reënforcement advanced to the support of the Union forces. At one time appearances seemed to indicate that the rebels were about to charge upon our feeble line, but a few well-directed volleys admonished them to remain behind their stone walls.

The Union artillery had thus far accomplished comparatively little, owing to its distance from the rebel works, and to the absence of all favorable positions where guns could be posted, on the Fredericksburg side of the river. Late in the afternoon, however, several guns took position in the upper streets of the city. The battle-field shook with their combined discharge. Meanwhile Hancock's division had been mostly withdrawn, to give place to the other division of the Second Corps. But many of the Twenty-seventh and other regiments remained at their posts, their safety being still more endangered if they attempted to leave the field.

At three o'clock in the afternoon, Howard's division advanced to the attack, to be hurled back before the overwhelming fire of the rebels. Only a brief time is now left before darkness will cover the scene. A final, desperate effort must be made to take the heights. Supported by the batteries in the streets, a fresh division advances into the field. How splendidly they charge! with what a perfect line! We can look into the faces of the men as they come on. Nothing apparently can withstand their onset. They come steadily to within a few paces of where we lie. Then bursts forth from the rebel works an iron tempest which had scarcely a parallel even on that day. Showers of bullets went whistling by or struck the ground in every direction, while pieces of shell, bits of old iron, grape and canister, rained down with a dull sound as they hit the earth. Arrested in its course, the line wavers, fires a few volleys, then scatters like chaff. It was now about dusk, and many of the Twenty-seventh who had remained on the field after the withdrawal of our division, retired into the city. At the edge of the plateau, where a battery was stationed, mounted officers were endeavoring to rally into some sort of order the shattered remnants of the division, whose magnificent charge we have just described.

The aspect of Fredericksburg that night cannot be adequately described. Lines of troops were under arms in the streets, ready to meet the enemy should they attempt to follow up their advantage and drive the army across the river. Crowds of soldiers, all excited by the events of the day, moved rapidly along the sidewalks. Processions of stretcher bearers tenderly conveyed their mangled freight to the hospitals. The eloquent red flag waved from almost every house, suggesting that the surgeons were diligently at work, while the glare of candles from the windows added to the wildness of the scene without.

The next day was the Sabbath, bright and clear overhead, but inexpressibly sad to us; for one third of the three hundred and seventy-five who followed the colors of the Twenty-seventh into battle, lay dead on the field, or wounded in the hospital. That forenoon was spent in cleaning our guns, in anticipation of further fighting. The Connecticut Brigade, under General Harland, was drawn up in line of battle on the main street, under orders to be ready at any moment to charge up the heights. As will subsequently appear, they were spared this perilous duty. Occasionally a resident of the town came timidly forth from his hiding-place, or a family, loaded down with bundles of household effects, slowly wended their way across the pontoon bridge, to escape the terrors surrounding them. A disagreeable uncertainty hung over every moment of the day, and when we awoke on the morning of the fifteenth, nothing had transpired to diminish our suspense. It was plain that something must be done, and that very soon. Delay only added to the difficulties of the situation. The army must fight, or evacuate the city. Every few minutes during the day we were ordered to fall in. The expectation was universal that we were again to be led to the attack. Hour after hour processions of ambulances moved across the pontoon bridge, and up the opposite bank, so that by evening the town was nearly empty of the wounded. General Burnside rode by and received a hearty welcome. Evidently a movement of some kind was soon to be made. A short time after dark the division was ordered under arms, and all, except the Twenty-seventh Connecticut, marched down Water street toward the railway bridge. Our little band stood waiting thus during the evening, in momentary expectation of being led out to support the pickets. At length orders were received to advance a few hundred yards below the railroad. As we arrived, the rest of the brigade silently arose from the ground where they had been sleeping, and like spectres vanished in the darkness. Here we remained until near midnight, obtaining what sleep was possible, then noiselessly fell in, and without a word spoken above a whisper, retired rapidly down the street to the pontoon bridge. The streets were as silent as death. A few soldiers were preparing to loosen the moorings which held the pontoons to the banks. After a brief halt, the Twenty-seventh, carrying a few boxes of ammunition, re-crossed the river by the same bridge on which they had entered the city four days before. On the road to Falmouth we met General Hancock, who asked, "What regiment is this?" and being informed, the Twenty-seventh Connecticut, expressed his great satisfaction with the conduct of the regiment in the events of the last few days. After losing our way in the darkness, and experiencing a heavy rain-storm, we arrived at our old camp ground on the morning of the sixteenth.

All unconscious of the night's events, the rebels threw a few shells into the town, and meeting no response, crept cautiously down from their fortifications, expecting to find our forces concealed under the banks of the river. But no pickets challenged their advance: the Union army had slipped from their grasp, the pontoons were up, and thus was accomplished one of the most skilful movements recorded in military history.

CHAPTER IV.
CAMP NEAR FALMOUTH.

The failure at Fredericksburg, considered in itself, and especially in connection with its causes, was well calculated to produce much discouragement throughout the entire army. On the eleventh of December the troops streamed forth from their camps, confident in their ability to drive the foe from Marye's Heights, and hurl him back to Richmond. On the sixteenth they returned, baffled and dispirited, having lost twelve thousand men in fruitless efforts to overcome the natural and artificial advantages of the rebel position. The fearful scenes of a battle may well impress the veteran of many conflicts; but when, for the first time, a regiment meets the enemy with every advantage in favor of the latter, and when the list of killed and wounded swells to unusual proportions, and nothing is accomplished by this expense of life and energy, it is no sign of weakness that despondency and gloom for a time prevail. Such a feeling, resulting from failure in the campaign, and from the loss of a large number of our most esteemed officers and men, pervaded the Twenty-seventh in common with the rest of the army. The loss of such men as Captains Schweizer and Taylor, Sergeants Barrett and Fowler, Corporals Mimmac and Alling, and many others, men of high character, who went to the field purely from a sense of duty—such men in their death could not fail to leave behind, among their fellow soldiers, a universal sorrow, reaching to the very depths of the heart. The memory of those who fell on the thirteenth of December, and many of whom lie in unknown graves back of Fredericksburg, will never lose its freshness, but rather grow in strength as the history of future years adds significance to the conflicts of the present.

Fortunately for the success of Burnside's plan of evacuation, his operations were concealed in the darkness of a severe storm, which had not terminated when we arrived in our former camp on the morning of the sixteenth. In the afternoon the two hundred and fifty men of the Twenty-seventh who had been picketing along the Rappahannock for the previous six days, rejoined us, many of them much exhausted by their unusually prolonged duties. Expecting to be absent from the regiment only a day, the ordinary limit of picket duty at one time, the party took with them only one day's rations, and in the confusion attending the movement of troops and the battle, rations for the additional time could be procured but irregularly and in insufficient quantities.

According to orders, the camp was now moved to a strip of pine woods skirting the west side of the division parade-ground. But this was not to be our permanent location; and after manœuvring for several days from one place to another, we at length encamped in the edge of a forest, only a few rods from where we first pitched our tents, on the line of the Rappahannock. An elevated plain stretched away between us and the river, and above a slight depression the clustered spires of Fredericksburg rose to view, from whose belfreys, on a Sabbath morning, we could sometimes hear the summons to the house of God. A walk of a few rods brought us in full view of the city, sitting in calm quiet among the hills, while long red lines told where the rebel earthworks lay, and little specks of white in the background disclosed the enemy's camps. Just under the edge of the bluff to our right, and concealed from view, was the village of Falmouth, a mongrel collection of houses arranged along dirty, unpaved streets.

Although intimations were thrown out that the army would now go into winter quarters, yet it was nearly two weeks before our men could dispossess themselves of the idea that some fine morning the old stereotyped order, "Strike tents and pack knapsacks!" would scatter to the winds their plans of personal comfort.

As soon as it was evident that no further movements would be made, the men vigorously applied themselves to the work of building huts, devoting the mornings to this labor, while brigade drill occupied the afternoon. In the hundred and thirty log houses of our little regimental village was embraced an amount of comfort wholly inconceivable by those who know nothing of the numerous contrivances a soldier's ingenuity can suggest to supply the place of ordinary conveniences. Generally, four congenial minds would unite their mechanical resources. A pine forest within reasonable distance, an axe and a shovel, one of Uncle Sam's mule teams, and a moderate degree of ingenuity, constitute the only capital of these camp carpenters. Having secured a favorable site, ten by seven, these comrades in bunk sally forth to the neighboring grove, and before their sturdy blows the old pines come crashing down, are split into slabs of the required length, and in due time reach their destination in camp. After smoothing the ground, and carefully removing stumps, the logs are hewn out and placed one above another, with the ends dove-tailed together, or set upright side by side in trenches, and soon the huts assume their full proportions—seven feet by ten. Every man now becomes a mason. The surrounding region is ransacked for stone and brick, with which to construct a fire-place at the front end. While this important work is going on, another is vigorously plying his wooden trowel, in plastering up the fissures with clay, on the principle that nothing is without its use, even Virginia mud. The roof is made of thin shelter-tents, buttoned together. As regards internal arrangements, at the further end are two bunks, one above the other; and as the upholsterer has not performed his part, and very likely never will, the occupants must content themselves with the soft side of pine slabs. On one side of the hut is a rack for the reception of guns and equipments, while at the other a cracker-box cover on stilts does duty as a table. In respect to seats, the ingenuity of different individuals showed itself in rudely constructed benches, or square boards, elevated on three-pronged crotchets, obtained in the woods, or was satisfied with the trunk of a tree cut into suitable lengths. Over the fire-place a mantle was generally located, containing a confused collection of tin plates and cups, knives and forks, and an endless variety of rubbish. In winter quarters it is very desirable to have a liberal supply of culinary furniture. The man whose fire-place is adorned with an iron frying-pan, is an object of envy to all his comrades, and is universally agreed to have reached the acme of comfort. However, the halves of old canteens, fitted with handles, answer very well in its place. In many of the huts, telegraph wire might be found doing service in the shape of a gridiron, upon which an occasional steak is broiled. Very likely, in its appropriate place is a coffee-pot, perhaps of the plantation style, two feet high, and large in proportion, which some argus-eyed soldier has observed and quietly confiscated.

Our huts were now nearly completed, and with no little satisfaction we surveyed their rough architecture, pork-barrel chimneys, and cracker-box doors, feeling that though the winds might blow, and the rainy season pour down its floods, we were prepared to endure it patiently. When the army has just completed its preparations for a comfortable time, it is safe to prophesy marching orders within three days thereafter. So it proved in the present instance. At dress parade, on the sixteenth of January, an order was read for the regiment to be ready to march on the next day with three days' rations. Details were dispatched at midnight to the Brigade Commissary's, after rations, and in good season on the seventeenth we were ready to start; but no final orders came, and it was bruited about that General J. E. B. Stuart, while roving around Dumfries and Alexandria with his rebel cavalry, in the absence of General Burnside in Washington, had telegraphed an order, as if from him, for the army to be ready to move. This is of a piece with a joke Stuart perpetrated on another occasion, when in the name of a Union General he telegraphed to Washington for certain stores, and is reported to have received them in good order.

On the eighteenth, Generals Burnside and Sumner reviewed our Army Corps. In the afternoon of the twentieth, an order was read, announcing that the army was "about to meet the enemy once more. The auspicious moment had arrived to strike a great and mortal blow at the rebellion, and to gain that decisive victory due to the country." The plan was for Hooker and Franklin to cross at Banks's Ford, six miles above Falmouth, and capture Taylor's Hill, the key of the position, from which they could advance in the rear of Fredericksburg, and turn the enemy's flank. This being done, Sumner with his grand division, to which the Twenty-seventh belonged, was to cross directly in front of the city at the old place, and take the batteries which had baffled our efforts in the battle of December thirteenth. The plan was substantially the same as the previous one, except that the flank movement was to be made upon the rebel left wing instead of his right. The failure of December resulted from the inefficiency of Franklin's flank demonstration, which allowed the enemy to mass his forces in front of Sumner. But now it was proposed to use two corps in the preliminary movement, and, provided they were successful in taking Taylor's Hill, Sumner's success would be assured, notwithstanding the rebels had been engaged for a month previous in strengthening and extending their works. Hooker and Franklin were in motion on the twentieth, while impetuous Sumner waited in his camps to hear the signal which should summon his veteran legions to the conflict. For several days, artillery and pontoons had been passing camp *en route* for Banks's Ford. If the weather continues favorable, the morrow will bring to our ears the boom of a hundred and fifty cannon.

But one of those strange events beyond man's power to avert disconcerts the whole plan. Instead of the roar of artillery, the unwelcome sound of rain salutes our ears the next morning, and continues for several days. Impassable roads, guns and pontoons fast in the mud, men toiling slowly along, or pulling at the boats, add a new page to the chapter of misfortune which had followed the noble Army of the Potomac. The rebels briefly summed up this last advance in these laconic words, "Burnside stuck in the mud!" which they impudently displayed from their picket-line, derisively inquiring when the "auspicious moment" would arrive. The rainy season had now set in in good earnest, and the wearied troops returned to their camps to await the advent of spring.

The progress of events had already foreshadowed a change of commanders, and on the twenty-ninth of January general orders were read announcing that General Burnside had been relieved, and the accession of Joe Hooker. The brief two months of Burnside's command had secured for him the sincere respect of the whole army. His honesty of purpose could not be impeached, and none felt more keenly than himself the ill success which had attended him. History, in summing up his campaign, will assign no small significance to the fact that Burnside did not receive the hearty coöperation of his subordinate commanders. He possessed an excessive self-distrust, and it was creditable to his candor to confess it; yet it is a question whether this distrust did not react unfavorably upon the officers and men of his command. Condemn it as we may, the boastful self-confidence of Hooker had no little influence in reïnspiring the army with that self-reliance which forms an important item in the calculations of success.

The advent of General Hooker was signalized by the abolition of the grand divisions, and a return to the simpler organization of *Corps d'Armée*. And what was of more consequence to the soldiers, an order was published directing the issue of four rations of fresh bread and fresh beef, and two rations of potatoes per week, with an occasional supply of other vegetables. This measure went right to the hearts of the army, for it must be confessed, and it is nothing to their disgrace, that the hearts of soldiers are very near, if not actually in, their stomachs. For an army is a great physical machine, expending a vast amount of animal power, and requiring careful attention to its animal wants to secure the highest moral efficiency.

From the battle of Fredericksburg to Hooker's move in the spring of 1863, the Twenty-seventh was engaged in picket duty along the Rappahannock, whose banks are as familiar to the men almost as the walks of childhood. Every other day, at seven in the morning, our quota of the division picket, equipped with blankets and one day's rations, formed in front of the Colonel's tent, and, after inspection, marched a mile to General Hancock's headquarters to undergo another inspection, after which a march of two or three miles brought them to the line of the river. The fact that three fourths of the time it was either rainy, or snowing, or cold and blustering, will give some idea of the arduous character of picket duty. By mutual agreement, the custom of picket firing, so annoying and useless, was discontinued, and friendly intercourse was no uncommon event; which latter practice, though harmless in itself, was yet so liable to make trouble that it was prohibited by special order. Frequently the rebels launched out on the river their diminutive craft, laden with tobacco and the latest Richmond papers, and bearing a note to "Gentlemen of the United States," requesting an interchange of commodities.

February twenty-second, we experienced the severest snow-storm of the season. At noon, through the thick mist of snow-flakes, came the deep boom of cannon, swelling into a loud chorus, from the adjacent batteries, answered by the low, muffled murmur of the distant discharge. In every direction salutes were being fired in honor of Washington's birthday. The time and place gave additional interest to this demonstration of respect for the Father of his Country, for this region is intimately connected with his history. Here he lived, and here are his descendants to this day, while on the other side of the Rappahannock a simple tomb marks his mother's resting-place.

March fifth, General Hooker reviewed the Second Army Corps, on a large plain, near Hancock's headquarters. The corps was drawn up in nine lines by brigade, in all nearly fifteen thousand men. General Hooker and General Couch, the then corps commander, with their brilliant and numerous staffs, rode rapidly up and down the several lines, while the men presented arms. Then taking position in front, the brigades marched by in column by company. Nothing was more impressive than the sight of the many regiments reduced to a mere fragment of their former strength—a silently eloquent commentary upon the inscriptions on their banners.

The rapid advance of spring, and Hooker's known determination to move on the enemy at the earliest possible moment, led to much speculation as to the plan of the new campaign. Before the close of March, intimations were thrown out that the army must expect soon to take the field. Daily balloon ascensions were made at several points on the river, in order to ascertain the position of the rebels. As an illustration of "Fighting Joe's" cool assurance, it was currently reported that one day he sent his balloon directly over the city of Fredericksburg, having previously notified the commandant that any molestation would meet with condign punishment from his batteries. The comparative nearness of our camp to the river afforded good opportunities for observing any change on the rebel side, and the probability that we should have to cross in front of the city in any future movement, whetted our curiosity. The rebels had been actively engaged all winter in strengthening their position, and now dark lines of rifle-pits and earthworks frowned from the bluffs for miles up and down the banks, commanding every available crossing. As may well be imagined, the prospect was by no means inviting.

CHAPTER V.
CHANCELLORSVILLE.

April eighth, the Twenty-seventh participated in the grand review of the Army of the Potomac by President Lincoln, preparatory to opening the spring campaign. Fifty or sixty thousand men were in line, and probably the army was never in better condition than at that time.

One week later, orders were received to supply the men with eight days' rations, five to be carried in their knapsacks, and three in their haversacks. Overcoats, dress coats, and everything which could possibly be dispensed with, were to be turned in to the Quartermaster. Each day company inspections were held, to see that the men were prepared as the orders directed. About this time the regiment was transferred to the Fourth Brigade, under the command of Colonel J. R. Brooke, of the Fifty-third Pennsylvania. A storm of two days' duration postponed the forward movement a short time, but by the twenty-seventh of the month the weather became tolerably settled, and now began a campaign which it was fondly hoped would result in the capture of Richmond. In the morning we sent out an additional picket of over three hundred men, leaving hardly a corporal's guard in camp. All day artillery and cavalry, pack-mules and wagon-trains, were passing camp, on their way to the right. Late in the evening, orders came to strike tents, pack up as quietly as possible, and report on the division parade at daybreak. Our pickets returned at two o'clock the next morning. The camp was now full of bustling preparation. The huts all illuminated; the eager hum of voices; men hurrying to and fro; the decided tones of command, combined to form a scene of excitement nowhere found but in the army. At daybreak the regiment fell in, and bade farewell to the dismantled camp, to enter upon an experience none of us had ever contemplated as likely to fall to our lot.

Camp near Falmouth will linger vividly in memory, when other more startling scenes of army life have faded into oblivion. Our four months' residence witnessed a complete change in the face of the country. A few stumps, or a solitary tree, were all that was left of the forests which, four months before, waved over a hundred square miles of territory. Here and there a house, tenantless, fenceless, and dingy, or a blackened ruin, with only a bare chimney standing, loomed above the naked landscape, a picture of complete desolation.

The division having assembled near General Hancock's headquarters, began the march for United States Ford, at seven in the morning. We passed many deserted encampments, whose late occupants, like ourselves, were on the move. Instead of following the direct course of the river up to the Ford, which was only ten miles above Falmouth, we pursued a very circuitous route, and, after an easy march, halted in a strip of woods, where we encamped for the night. The next day, at evening, we had just pitched our tents and built fires, and were in the act of making coffee, and frying a bit of pork or beef, when the order came for the Twenty-seventh to fall in with all possible dispatch. Suppers were thrust into haversacks, without much regard to order, and in a few moments the regiment marched off about a mile, to picket in the woods. This duty occupied us until the next afternoon, when we were relieved, and hastened on to overtake the rest of the brigade, which had already broken camp. During the night previous a light fall of rain took place, just enough, however, to put the roads in bad condition. All along the route, pioneers were thrown out in advance, to corduroy the worst places for the passage of the trains. As far as the eye could reach, a continuous line of army wagons filled the road, urging their way forward with the greatest difficulty. The woods on either hand rang with the sharp crack of the teamsters' whips, and simultaneously a chorus of wild shouts burst from the driver and the men pushing at the wheels, while high above the din rose shrill cries, resembling the notes of the screech-owl. Then, with a quick, jerking jump, the nimble mules landed the team in the next rut, to await the reception of the same magical sounds.

Advancing to within a short distance of the Ford, the corps halted to await the completion of the preparations for crossing. The sun now burst forth from the canopy of clouds as if in glad sympathy with the exhilaration which pervaded all hearts in consequence of the encouraging news from the front. A dispatch from General Hooker announced that the success of the Fifth, Eleventh, and Twelfth Corps was all that could be desired, and that the rebels were retiring. These corps broke camp early on Monday morning, April twenty-seventh, and took the route to Kelly's Ford, twenty-five miles above Fredericksburg. The pontoons were laid and a crossing effected on the following day, with very little opposition, and the troops pushed forward rapidly to Germania Ford, on the Rapidan, for the purpose of concentrating at Chancellorsville. General Stoneman, with his cavalry, crossed on Wednesday, to enter upon the grand raid which the *Richmond Examiner* characterized as the "most audacious enterprise of the war." The diversion from Germania caused the rebels to evacuate their works in front of the United States Ford, so that no molestation was offered when the pontoons were laid for the passage of the Second Corps. Late in the afternoon of April thirtieth, we moved rapidly down the abrupt, woody bank, and once more, set foot on the south side of the Rappahannock. A line of well-constructed rifle-pits, with more elaborate works for cannon, at intervals of several hundred yards, commanded the crossing. In their hasty retreat the rebels left behind two pieces of artillery spiked. Only a few miles now separated us from the scene of operations, and after marching through woods, and over muddy roads, rendered infinitely worse by the constant passage of troops, we bivouacked for the night a short distance from the Chancellor House, a large brick mansion, so called from its occupant, V. Chancellor. This residence was situated about five miles from United States Ford, and about ten miles southwest of Fredericksburg, at the junction of the plank road to Gordonsville and the Orange County turnpike. A shapeless mass of ruins is all that now remains of what gave name to one of the most remarkable battles of the war.

Save an occasional discharge of cannon, the forenoon of May first was spent in comparative quiet, neither party seeming disposed to inaugurate the conflict. Movements, however, were in progress with a view to ascertain the enemy's position. In the afternoon the Twenty-seventh participated in a reconnoissance for this purpose, which came very near proving an affair of no little importance. Leaving our bivouack in the woods, we advanced down the road by the Chancellor House, and ascending a gentle elevation, turned aside into an open lot on the left, near a small dwelling, afterward occupied by General Lee as his headquarters. Here a section of artillery was exchanging compliments in a lively manner with a rebel battery, a short distance up the road. Several companies were immediately deployed as skirmishers, with the remainder as a support, and advanced through the woods to feel the enemy's position, and develop his strength. Suddenly the artillery limbered up, the skirmishers were called in, and the reconnoitering force retired to the rear at double-quick. This movement was rendered necessary by an advance of the enemy, seriously threatening our right flank; but they were foiled in the attempt, and fell back before a stubborn fire of musketry and artillery. For a few moments we remained in line of battle in the open ground near the Chancellor House, then, moving down the road a short distance, deployed through the thick and tangled woods on the left. Appearances indicated that the rebels were about to charge down from the ridge from which we had just retired, but they contented themselves with shelling us furiously with their batteries. Long before the cannonade ceased, the mellow twilight of a May evening had passed into the darkness of night, adding to the fearful sublimity of the scene, as the rebel guns woke the sleeping forest echoes, and shells careered wildly through the air, and crashed among the trees. Quietly resting on the ground, we wait for the iron storm to pass. No sooner has the last shell swept over our heads and burst into numberless fragments, than we enter upon the night's work, of intrenching our position against the anticipated attack of the morrow. The rebels were apparently engaged in similar work just across the ravine. It was a busy and exciting scene along the lines of the army that night. The rapid strokes of axemen, followed by the dull sound of falling trees, rang through the woods in every direction. Details of men were at hand to put the logs in position, while others dug a trench in the rear, and heaped the soil upon them. For some distance in front of the breastworks, trees were cut down for the purpose of obstructing the enemy's advance. After the completion of our intrenchments, we rested under arms, and at daybreak, May second, as silently as possible, marched out into the road, and past the Chancellor House, and took a new position in Hooker's line of battle. The rebels soon entered the place we had just left, which, however, was of very little value to them, and could easily be reöccupied when circumstances required. We spent the forenoon in building breastworks, while on the other parts of the line there was much skirmishing, and several sharp fights. At intervals during the day the enemy opened upon us with shot and shell, discovering our position by the smoke curling above the trees from the camp fires. At noon, when rations were being dealt out to the companies, the rebel gunners, doubtless tantalized by the display, seemed determined to involve commissaries and rations in one common ruin.

Several days had now passed in the usual preliminaries to a battle. Hooker had succeeded in drawing the main force of the rebels from their works in the rear of Fredericksburg, and was himself well intrenched in the dense woods skirting the plank road, and most appropriately called the Wilderness. The line of battle of the Union forces formed a broad wedge, whose base rested on the Rappahannock, the apex terminating at the extreme front beyond the Chancellor House. The Eleventh Corps held the extreme right, and next in order were the Third, Twelfth, and Second, while the Fifth occupied the left.

Lee is said to have issued orders to his troops to break this line, at all hazards. A brief calm followed the desultory movements of the day. The men stood in their places behind the breastworks, gazing into the woods in front, eagerly listening to hear the first sound which should tell where the rebel blow would strike. At four o'clock in the afternoon, the enemy advanced in heavy force down the plank road, and began the attack in the neighborhood of the intrenchments we had thrown up the night before. The rapid fire of musketry on our right indicated a serious attempt to pierce the centre of the Union line. Under cover of this movement, the indomitable Jackson advanced his hordes through the woods, and hurled their solid array on Hooker's right wing, directly in rear of our present position. Let the Eleventh Corps stand firm, and victory will rest on our banners ere the close of day. The current history of the hour tells us how the crisis was met. But more expressive than history itself was the wild shout of triumph that burst from one end of the rebel line to the other, as it swept over the earthworks, and saw the panic-stricken corps dashing madly to the rear. Who can describe the almost breathless interest with which we listened to the fluctuations of the conflict? Now the avalanche of the enemy is stayed a moment in its course; then nearer and nearer approaches the sound of battle, and it seems as if the next instant the foe will dash in upon our rear. A portion of the Second Corps hurries away to the scene of strife, and General Hancock, every nerve strung to the highest pitch of excitement, rides up to inform the Colonel that probably we should not be called into action, but were to hold our position, and that in case of necessity we could fight on either side of our breastworks, plainly pointing to the possibility that the enemy may attack in the rear. Through the woods behind us we can see batteries of artillery rushing into position near Hooker's headquarters, and in a few moments the forest trembles with the terrific cannonade, vying with the thunders of heaven in the compass of its sound. In the distance the deep, prolonged boom of a hundred-pounder swells the bass notes of the chorus. Double-shotted with grape and canister, the field-pieces sweep the rebel line with murderous effect. At length darkness put an end to this sublime exhibition of human power. The frightened whippoorwills ceased their plaintive cries; the quiet moon rose over the bloody field, and Nature sank into a silence fairly oppressive. We remained under arms most of the night, frequently changing our position as the emergency required.

At eleven o'clock occurred one of those episodes of warfare which, in startling grandeur and terrible magnificence, well-nigh border on the supernatural. The forces of Hooker and Lee were resting on their arms, renewing their energies with an hour of broken slumber, and ready to rush to battle at the first flash of dawn. The air was perfectly still and serene, transmitting the rays of the moon with unusual brilliancy. Scarcely a sound disturbed the painful silence of the almost interminable woods. All at once the artillery, massed on the ridge hardly half a mile behind us, with one tremendous crash poured in its fire upon the enemy's position, covering the charge of a division of infantry. The thunder of musketry and artillery reverberated through the forest with an effect inconceivably grand.

At the earliest moment on Sabbath morning, May third, the battle was renewed, but apparently with less vigor than on the preceding day, and yet, as brigade after brigade became engaged, and the almost unexampled roar of musketry rolled along the line, it was evident that the enemy were about to follow up, with even greater desperation, the advantage already gained. Immediately after breakfast, the Twenty-seventh, with the exception of two companies—D and F, engaged in other duty—was ordered down into the intrenchments we had thrown up, near the apex of the wedge, the Friday night previous. These works now formed a part of the picket-line of the army, and from the nature of the position and its relation to the movements of the enemy, a large force was required in order to hold it. As is usual in such cases, when a picket in force is ordered, the colors did not accompany the column. As the regiment advanced, at double-quick, down the hill into the ravine, it was met by a heavy fire of musketry. A number were wounded, and several shot through the head, just as they entered the breastworks. One or two regiments whose ammunition was exhausted, were gradually drawn off in small squads. Not succeeding in their first attempt, the rebels made no further attack in force upon our part of the line, but, concealed in the thick woods, continually annoyed us with a scattering fire. The men replied as they had opportunity, and with considerable effect, as the rebels themselves afterward acknowledged. Colonel Bostwick was particularly noticeable for the almost reckless exposure of himself to the enemy's fire, while attending to his duties at different points in the line. Lieutenant-Colonel Merwin reminded him several times of the great danger he incurred, as he stood on a slightly rising ground to the rear of the rifle-pits, a conspicuous object for some rebel bullet.

While the conflict was culminating in other parts of the field, the enemy in our immediate front were not so idle as appearances indicated. Looking through the woods, we could indistinctly see a large body of infantry making a wide circuit to the right, seemingly with a view to attack some remote part of the line. A similar movement took place also to the left. "Look out on the right!" "Look out on the left!" passed up and down the line, and every man was on the alert, ready to meet them should they attempt to carry our intrenchments.

Suddenly, from unseen batteries behind us, comes a deep roar, and the next moment shell after shell shrieks through the trees and bursts almost in the rifle-pits. The thought flashes upon us that the rebels are in our rear, but is dismissed with the reflection that it is only a Union battery firing too low, and will soon correct its false range. Meanwhile our little band had been reduced to less than four hundred men, embracing two hundred and seventy of the Twenty-seventh, with small portions of the One Hundred and Forty-fifth Pennsylvania and Second Delaware; and this force being entirely inadequate to hold the extended line, Colonel Bostwick dispatched Major Coburn to General Hancock for reënforcements. In a few moments the shelling ceased, and far up the road in front appeared a rebel officer waving a flag of truce, and slowly advancing, waiting for a recognition. The men stopped firing in the immediate vicinity of the road, while for a moment the musketry became more brisk on the left flank. At length the rebel officer arrived within a few paces of the works, where he was halted, to await the presence of Colonel Morris, of the Sixty-sixth New-York, commanding the whole line. This officer was not to be found, and the responsibility of receiving the communication from the flag of truce devolved upon Colonel Bostwick, of the Twenty-seventh. The rebel—a tall, rough specimen, and yet with the manner of a gentleman—announced himself as Lieutenant Bailey, of a Georgia regiment; that he had been sent to inform us that we were entirely surrounded; that there was no possible avenue of escape, and therefore he summoned us to surrender, and thus avoid the loss of life which would inevitably follow any resistance to the overwhelming force in front and rear. The Colonel replied that he did not "see" it, and proceeded to investigate the actual state of affairs. Meanwhile Lieutenant-Colonel Merwin went up through the woods in the rear only to find it too true that the rebels were posted in strong force, to bar any escape in that direction. Masses of the enemy pouring in on the right and left, revealed at once the desperate position in which we were placed, while the singing bullets from the woods behind as well as in front, indicated that the foe were closing in upon us. The first impulse among officers and men was to attempt to force our way through. But it was evident that such a course would result in the destruction of more than half our number, while the remainder would inevitably fall into the hands of the enemy. After a hurried consultation among the officers, a surrender was agreed upon, and the formality had hardly been completed, when a heavy line of rebel skirmishers swept out of the woods behind. Only five minutes before, the men stood at their posts undisturbed by even a doubt of their security; now, astonished at the sudden *denouement*, we found ourselves about to enter upon the terrible uncertainties of rebel captivity. And this surprise and mortification was increased by the conviction that serious disaster must have overtaken the Union army. The history of the day establishes the fact, that Saturday's misfortune, and the subsequent operations of Sunday morning, compelled the formation of a new line of battle. The surging conflict had gradually crowded Hooker back, and late in the afternoon the army retired, by his order, to a position some distance in rear of the Chancellor House. As General Hancock afterward stated, orders were sent down to the Twenty-seventh to fall back at the same time, but they failed to reach us; and while the rest of the army had retreated to the new line, the Twenty-seventh still remained at the extreme front of the old, entirely unconscious of this change of position. Our situation in a ravine, surrounded by dense woods, rendered it impossible to observe the movements going on in other parts of the extended field. The enemy, already aware of Hooker's withdrawal, immediately planted a battery behind us, supported, as one of the rebels afterward said, by two brigades of infantry.

The experience of Major Coburn immediately after the shelling, while *en route* to deliver the Colonel's request to General Hancock, more than confirms this statement. On his way to the rear he was accompanied by one of our sergeants, severely wounded in the early part of the action. They had passed hardly half a mile through the woods when they were taken prisoners, and the Major was conducted into the road, where he found a large part of Stonewall Jackson's corps, under command of Major-General Anderson. Already they had formed their skirmish line and were crowding forward with all possible speed, certain of their prey. Outnumbered on every hand, and with batteries in front and rear, it would have been madness to have attempted to force our way through in the face of such odds. The gallant Brooke, with characteristic bravery, when he heard the firing, volunteered to charge down with his brigade to our relief, but General Hancock refused permission, for fear of bringing on a general engagement while the army was changing its position.

CHAPTER VI.
ON TO RICHMOND.

Let us now return to the little band of prisoners in that woody ravine. As soon as the surrender had been consummated the men threw away their guns, many of them with the cartridges, into a rivulet near the intrenchments, and some cut up their equipments, determined to afford as little aid and comfort to the rebels as possible. Our newly-made acquaintances exhibited a most remarkable *penchant* for cutlery and other conveniences Yankees are always supposed to have in their possession. One of the rebel skirmishers had hardly lowered his gun from an aim, when he walked up to one of our men and said: "Have you got a knife to sell?" "No;" and somewhat abashed, he went off to try his luck in a more promising field. We were now ordered to fall in, and a part were marched up the road to General Lee's headquarters, where the rebels took away our knapsacks, rubber blankets, shelter-tents, and canteens, and registered our names. Quite a crowd of butternuts assembled to view the "Yanks" and prosecute their schemes of trade.

While we were near headquarters, a General of high rank rode up, unattended by his staff, and was received among his soldiers with a style of cheering or yelling peculiar to themselves. The rebel chief seemed lost in deep thought, scarcely noticing the squad of prisoners or the cheers of his men. The signs of care were strongly marked upon his iron countenance. Clad in simple garb, with no prominent badge of distinction, calm and determined in demeanor, stood before us the commander of the Army of Northern Virginia, the military pillar of the rebellion. The General hurriedly retired into his quarters, and our attention was attracted by a motley array of rebel soldiery marching up the road. Could we have forgotten the stern realities of our situation, we might well have regarded the display as a military burlesque. On a closer inspection, we found the butternut phalanx to be composed of tall, lank specimens of "poor white trash," with hats slouched in the most approved style, and knapsacks of every conceivable variety. The officers were, many of them, equipped with swords of a most ancient description, which had already filled a term of service in the olden time. Here is a man with a very good blanket, and we soon see the letters U.S. displayed under the folds, while on another back is strapped an old piece of carpet. A more dirty, seedy, ill-favored, border-ruffian, ignorant set of men we had never met before, and this is just the material for an efficient army, marshalled in defence of treason and slavery.

The preparations were now completed, and under a strong guard we started off for Spottsylvania Court-House. The roads were full of Confederate wounded, moving to the rear. Our route crossed a section of the battle-field, but all was now quiet; only splintered trees and lines of breastworks told of the fierce conflicts of the last few days. At dusk we entered the now historic town of Spottsylvania, and passed the night within the inclosure of the Court-House. A portion of the regiment remained in the vicinity of the battle ground, and did not reach the village until the following afternoon. On the morning of May fourth we resumed our march for Guinea's Station, a small hamlet on the Richmond and Fredericksburg railroad, important as a dépôt of supplies for Lee's army. Here seemed to be the general rendezvous of prisoners, and fifteen hundred had already been assembled previous to our arrival. Near the station was the house where Stonewall Jackson lay wounded and afterward died, an event which clothed the whole Confederacy in mourning. Our stay at Guinea's Station was prolonged until Thursday, May seventh—three days of misery, hardly paralleled in any of the experiences of the whole nine months' campaign. Tuesday dawned upon us intensely hot. The broiling rays of the sun seemed to concentrate upon the large open lot occupied by the Union prisoners, unrelieved even by a solitary tree. Later in the day a terrific thunder shower burst upon us, passing at length into a settled storm, bitterly raw and cold, continuing all night and the next day at short intervals. The rain poured in torrents, flowing in streams across the lot. A ludicrous sight, indeed, were the nearly two thousand shelterless men, emphatically squatter sovereigns, scattered about over the field in speechless resignation, drenched through and through in the pelting storm.

Thus far we had subsisted on the scanty remains of Uncle Sam's rations. "What a fall was there!" when we descended from Joe Hooker's generous hospitality to the frugal fare doled out to us by the rebel commissary. A brief residence at one of Jeff.'s hotels is an infallible remedy for all who are disposed to grumble at army food. The order is given, "Fall in for rations!" We had almost concluded that this order would never again greet our ears until we should once more stand under the flag of the Union. Immediately our thoughts recurred to camp near Falmouth, and in imagination floated visions of beef, pork, hard-tack, fresh bread—in fact, Uncle Sam's army ration loomed up in bolder relief than ever before. In silent suspense we advance and receive—three pints of flour apiece. The inquiry arose, What shall we do with it? Our extremely limited culinary facilities soon settled that question. There was but one alternative, and the men immediately built little fires and were busily engaged in cooking up a bill of fare for the march to Richmond, said bill of fare consisting simply of flour and water mixed together and dried before the fire. A New-England farmer would regard it as a personal insult if one should offer such stuff to his hogs. Even a swill-carrier would indignantly protest.

Many suggestive sights fed our curiosity. Processions of trains were constantly coming and going from the station, transporting supplies for Lee's army. Shabby army wagons—regular Noah's arks mounted on wheels—

horses and mules reduced to mere skin and bone—every thing foreshadowed the ruin of the Confederacy. Thursday morning, May seventh, we began the march for Richmond, escorted by the Twelfth South Carolina. The roads were in an awful condition, in consequence of recent rains. On the route we passed through Bowling Green, a few miles east of the railroad, and by evening reached Milford Station. Just beyond the village we were obliged to wade the Mattapony river, and halted for the night in a forest near by. After a toilsome march, we bivouacked, on Friday evening, a short distance beyond Hanover Station. At this place each man received five medium-sized crackers and an ounce of bacon. Our guards were very incommunicative, but occasionally sung out, "Git in yer groups of fours dar!" or ventured an "I reckon," or a "right smart."

May ninth seemed to concentrate and intensify all previous discomforts. The day was exceedingly hot, and our route lay through a succession of vile swamps, skirting the Pamunkey and Chickahominy rivers, and extending to within four or five miles of Richmond. Here the ground is somewhat higher, and pleasant villas nestle among the trees, now just assuming the verdure of spring. As we passed one of these residences, the proprietor—an old gentleman—and the women turned out *en masse* to view the procession. No doubt we did present a rather sorry plight; at any rate, these high-bred F. F. V.'s laughed exultingly, and were loud and profuse in their remarks, complimentary to Yankees in general and us in particular. "Oh! well, you have got to Richmond now!" screeched out one of them with all the impotent ire she could muster. "Next time we are coming with guns," was the reply. "Yes, yes," chimed in the old man, "we saw a lot of you fellows last summer over there," pointing with his cane in the direction of McClellan's achievements in the Chickahominy swamps. Thus a running fire of words was kept up all along the line.

We could now see in the distance the spires of the rebel capital. Just outside the city, lines of earthworks, with here and there a frowning cannon, commanded the road. Our flattering reception thus far in the villages along the route from Guinea's Station led us to expect even greater demonstrations from the Richmond populace. As we entered the city, it seemed as if all Richmond had turned out to view the Yankee parade. The streets in the suburbs were full of people—men, women, and children, whites, negroes, mulattoes—all in one confused crowd, and swayed for the most part with clamorous exultation; while "her beauty and her chivalry," arm in arm, gloated over the scene with a kind of fiendish delight. One old woman, raising her arms in blank astonishment, screamed out: "Why, all Hooker's army is coming!" We thought to ourselves, she is about right; Hooker's army will be here one of these days, and with guns too. "What have you come down here for?" demanded one, whose very countenance flashed vengeance.

"Oh! we are only Hooker's advance guard, come down to act as pall-bearers at Stonewall Jackson's funeral," some one quietly replied. In his rage he answered: "If you were not a prisoner, I'd shoot you down." "You've got to Richmond in a way you didn't expect." "See these Yanks; there's hardly an honest face among 'em all." "What a hang-dog look!" These, and many other expressions, of all degrees of refinement, were launched at us. It really seemed as if the chivalry had studied for this very occasion some vocabulary of Billingsgate, and practiced it beforehand, so as to get it off in the most approved style of grimace and tone. Although Richmond was the Sodom and Gomorrah of treason, and the concentrated essence of rebel villainy and venom, we were not left entirely to this dark view of the picture. While we stood in the street, just before entering Jeff.'s hotel, a German woman, in the kindness and, I believe, loyalty of her heart, came hurriedly out from a neighboring house with a large loaf of cake, and divided it up among the eager men. She then went back, but soon returned, laden with a lot of bread, which she distributed in like manner. Several other instances of similar character occurred, like flashes of golden sunlight in a dark and lowering sky.

Wearied by the day's march and its exciting scenes, and exhausted through want of food, most of the men were now ushered into a tobacco factory belonging to Crew and Pemberton, and situated on Carey street, opposite the infamous Libby prison, of which it is a counterpart. More than a thousand men were stowed away in Crew and Pemberton's factory, an average of nearly three hundred in each story. Two hundred and eighty-nine, including the larger part of the Twenty-seventh, occupied the upper loft, and when all reclined upon the floor almost every square foot was covered. Many were so thoroughly exhausted as to be unable to drag themselves up-stairs without assistance from their comrades. Also, Belle Island welcomed a small number to its sands and wild onions. Forty or fifty of the men were assigned to Libby prison, where were already quartered the commissioned officers of the Twenty-seventh. The latter had arrived in Richmond a day or two previous, after a journey in crowded cars from Guinea's Station. The people residing in the vicinity of the route seemed in a perfect ferment of vindictive excitement, and gathered here and there in boisterous groups to gaze at the unusual pageant. The Virginia women were especially spiteful, in word and demeanor. Some of them, perched in conspicuous places, waved little Confederate flags, as if to attract the more attention, and shouted out, "That's what's the matter!" "Come on, you cursed rascals!" "Have you got Old Abe with you?" "Ain't you a sweet-looking party?" The usual miscellaneous assemblage greeted them as they alighted in Broad street, and seemed very eager to remind them of their advent in the rebel capital. "Well, you've got here, have you?" "How do you like the place?" "You're a sweet-looking crowd of thieves, aren't you?" Thus they were escorted to Libby, and handed over to the tender mercies of Captain Turner and his assistants, who searched the prisoners, and appropriated all contraband articles.

The day following the arrival of the main body of the regiment was the Sabbath, just one week since we fell into rebel hands. During this week all the rations each man received from the rebel authorities amounted to three pints of flour, five medium-sized crackers, and an ounce or two of bacon. All day Sunday the men were clamorous for something to eat. The guards about the prison were under strict orders to prevent the people from selling any thing to the prisoners, but, notwithstanding this, some articles did pass the blockade. At evening, the rebels distributed to every four men what purported to be a four-pound loaf of bread, and a pound of pork. Less than three pounds of bread would be nearer the truth, making about ten or twelve ounces for each man, and this with three ounces of pork formed the daily ration for one person. As far as it went, it was very good. Every morning the prison director, with the rank of major, and his clerk, a renegade New-Yorker—precious scoundrels both of them—came into the prison to count us over, and see if we were all there.

Thus affairs continued for several days—the same dull routine of prison life, varied by nothing except the contraband reading of Richmond papers, with accounts of Stonewall Jackson's funeral, at which there was great joy in Libby. At length, on Wednesday morning, came the glad announcement that the United States transports were at City Point, awaiting our arrival. The rebel officers administered to us the following paroling oath: "We, the undersigned, do solemnly swear and pledge our sacred word, that we will not, during the existing hostilities between the United States and the Confederate States of America, aid or abet the enemies of said Confederate States, by arms or otherwise, until regularly and legally exchanged, or otherwise released. So help me God. And we do acknowledge our names appended to the same, as though signed by ourselves." At half-past three in the afternoon, with gladness indescribable, we left those prison walls, to enter upon the march to City Point, a place about thirty-five miles from Richmond. Crossing the James river into Manchester, we took the turnpike road to Petersburg, under the escort chiefly of cavalry. The rebels hurried us forward for miles almost at double-quick, without any halt. As Major Turner rode by, the men called to him for a rest. He shouted out, "There is no rest for the wicked!" and passed on.

It was the purpose of our escort to continue the march all night, but a thunder-storm of surpassing violence seriously interfered. A darkness, so intense that we could not see a foot before us, enveloped the road. Slowly, through mud, and rain, and darkness, we straggled along, until near midnight. It was impossible to go further. Scattered along the roadside for miles were hundreds too much exhausted to keep up with the column, and finally we all dragged ourselves into the marshy woods, and, lulled to sleep by the babbling brooks flowing around us in every direction, forgot awhile the fatigue of the march. At an early hour the next day the weary column again moves on, each man sustaining his waning strength by frequent halts. Petersburg is passed, and ten miles more of mud. At length the waters of the James river glimmer in the distance; the old flag, floating proudly at the masthead of the Union transports, beckons onward. The men attempt to cheer, but it dies on their lips; nature is too much exhausted to utter the feelings which swell all hearts. With renewed energy we press forward, and soon enter the deserted village of City Point, whose shattered roofs tell of a former bombardment. That march from Richmond to City Point stands almost unexampled in the whole experience of the Twenty-seventh. Many were ready to drop on the ground from utter inability to go further. Behind them frowned the grim, historic walls of Libby; dreary months of incarceration moved by in slow procession, crowded full with the records of cruelty, and starvation, and disease; while forward to freedom and humanity, forward to generous care and protection, written on every fold of the old flag, fired them with new determination to toil on. Once more they stand on a Union deck, resolved to strike a heavier blow for their country when again they advance to meet her barbarous foes. As soon as the men were aboard the transports, a supply of food was distributed to meet their pressing wants. The steamers quietly dropped down the beautiful James river, bordered with high banks, rich in the fresh verdure of spring, with here and there a handsome villa peering above the trees. We anchored for the night at Harrison's Landing, an important point in the history of the Peninsular campaign. The next forenoon our transports steamed into Hampton Roads. Hampton, once the summer resort of the Virginia chivalry, Newport News, the distant spires of Norfolk, the topmast of the Cumberland still pointing skyward, the little monitors, and the Rip-Raps, and that grand old sentinel, Fortress Monroe, all crowd on the view as we round to at Old Point Comfort. A brief stop, and we are off again for Annapolis, where we arrive on the morning of May sixteenth, and are quartered in barracks in the rear of the town. After three days of rest, we start for Alexandria, by way of Chesapeake Bay and the Potomac, and on May twenty-first are introduced within the narrow precincts of Convalescent Camp.

The majority of the officers were detained in Richmond several days after the departure of the privates. Meanwhile, the rebels had been threatening retaliation for General Burnside's execution of two spies, in Kentucky; and the officials in charge of Libby took great delight in telling our officers that they were to have tickets in the lottery, which would determine the victims of the *lex talionis*. A few days later, they were relieved of their suspense by the announcement that the lot had fallen upon two officers from Tennessee. This affair having been arranged satisfactorily to the rebel authorities, the officers of the Twenty-seventh received their parole early Saturday morning, May twenty-third, and started in freight cars for City Point, and from that place were transported, *via* Fortress Monroe, to Annapolis, where they arrived on the morning of the twenty-fifth.

Leaving the paroled prisoners of the Twenty-seventh to endure as best they can the idleness and discontent of Convalescent Camp, let us return in thought to the wilds of Chancellorsville, and from those scenes of the third of May follow the little band which still remains at the front, to bear our flag to victory on the heights of Gettysburg. Eight companies were captured on that memorable May morning; but D and F, having been detached for duty elsewhere, escaped this unexpected misfortune, and fell back with the main army, when General Hooker retired to his new line of battle. Meanwhile, the duties of these remnants of the regiment were somewhat disconnected. During Saturday night following the disaster of the Eleventh Corps, Company A had been out on picket duty, and were relieved by Company D, at an early hour the next morning, in time to accompany the main body of the regiment to the place where they were captured. Company F had been previously detached to fill up a gap in the line between the Fifty-third and One Hundred and Forty-fifth Pennsylvania, and were soon after ordered up to the Chancellor House to support the famous Pettit's battery. Here they remained until Sunday afternoon, under a severe fire. Twice the rebels charged up in solid masses, but were repulsed before Pettit's rapid and irresistible volleys. In the evening of that day Company F went out on picket, and continued in this duty until the following Monday night. It was on this part of the line that Stonewall Jackson received his mortal wound.

It will be remembered that when the regiment went down to the picket-line that Sabbath morning, the colors remained behind by order of General Brooke. Although the rifle-pits were now entirely deserted, the color-guard, having no orders to leave, maintained their position until ten A.M., much of the time under a severe shelling. At that hour they were ordered to the rear, and soon after joined Company D, which was the last to leave the old picket-line of the army, as stated by the staff officer who brought to them the orders to fall back. The various remnants of the Twenty-seventh were not reünited until a late hour on Monday.

The conflict of Sabbath morning, May third, terminated at eleven o'clock, and, with the exception of a feeble demonstration by Jackson's forces in the afternoon, the remainder of the day passed in comparative quiet. Meanwhile, Hooker had contracted his lines, and the army was now massed within a nearly equilateral triangle, its base resting upon the Rappahannock. The Eleventh and Twelfth Corps occupied the side facing Fredericksburg. On the side looking toward the Rapidan were the First, Third, and Fifth, while our Second corps was formed in four compact lines at the angle, which was open ground about a two-story white house, on the Ely's Ford road, near the junction with that leading to United States Ford. This was a strong position, favorable for artillery, and justly regarded as the most important in the whole line. The Twenty-seventh held a position to the left of the white house, where General Hooker now had his headquarters. Such continued to be the situation of the army during the succeeding two days. The enemy seemed disinclined to venture a general attack, but occasionally shelled our intrenchments, as if to reassure themselves that Hooker was still there. Affairs could not remain long in this doubtful state. The golden opportunity to crush the rebels, when the thunder of Sedgwick's cannon, advancing from Fredericksburg, filled the breezes with the murmuring notes of success, had passed, and now every hour of delay added to the swelling torrent of the Rappahannock, threatening to sweep away the feeble threads which connected the army with its supplies.

Monday evening, May fourth, General Hooker held a council of war, which decided that it was best to withdraw the army the following night. Accordingly, eight o'clock, Tuesday evening, was the hour fixed upon; but the troops did not begin to move until after midnight, in consequence of a heavy storm, which carried away some of the bridges. The Twenty-seventh remained under arms all night, in the rain, with orders to be ready to start at any moment. At length, at four in the morning of May sixth, the regiment fell back with the rest of the brigade, re-crossed at United States Ford, and, after a march of twelve hours, arrived at the old camp, near Falmouth. The Sixty-fourth New-York were found quietly ensconced in the few huts which the scavengers of Falmouth had left standing, and demurred somewhat at leaving their grateful shelter, but finally recognized the prior claim of the Twenty-seventh. After a few days, the regiment changed its camp to a more healthy location two miles further back from the river. The losses of Hooker's campaign had reduced our numbers from nearly four hundred men to one hundred and sixty, embracing D and F, and small squads of other companies, the whole under command of the senior officer, Captain Joseph R. Bradley, of Company F. Dress parades took place as usual, and duty at the old picket-line on the Rappahannock was resumed, bearing very heavily upon our diminished ranks. Occasionally the rebel pickets shouted across the river to know where the Twenty-seventh Connecticut had gone, and in the same breath gave the answer, "To picket around Richmond." On the thirteenth of May, several of our wounded men came over from Fredericksburg, having been nine days in the rebel hospitals.

After the battle of Chancellorsville, General D. N. Couch, the corps commander, was relieved at his own request, and our division general, W. S. Hancock, justly characterized as the very impersonation of war, succeeded to the command. As soon as possible, after the return of our commissioned officers from Richmond, a part were exchanged, and at the earliest moment Colonel Bostwick returned to the front, followed by Lieutenant-Colonel Merwin, Major Coburn, and Lieutenants Frank Chapman, Burdict, Rice, Muhlner, and Cross, who rejoined the regiment on the eleventh of June. Colonel Bostwick, being prevented from remaining with his men, in consequence of a severe and protracted sickness, the Lieutenant-Colonel took command of the battalion, which now consisted of three companies, an additional one having been formed from the remnants of the captured companies, and placed under command of Captain Jedediah Chapman.

CHAPTER VII.
GETTYSBURG.

The result of the battle of Chancellorsville determined General Lee to carry out his cherished plan of invading the North. Hooker's position in front of Fredericksburg being unfavorable for attack, the rebel chief early in June began a series of movements with the view of drawing him away from the river. Leaving Hill's corps in the works at Fredericksburg, to keep up appearances, he concentrated Ewell's, Longstreet's, and Hood's forces at Culpepper Court-House, near the upper waters of the Rappahannock, and about the middle of June pushed forward rapidly into the Shenandoah Valley, and either captured or defeated the feeble Union force opposing his march. Meanwhile, Hooker's watchful eye was upon him, and the Sixth Corps crossed the river just below Fredericksburg to determine the strength and intentions of the rebels. A few days later, several army corps broke camp, and started off in the direction of Warrenton, for the purpose of watching the movements of the enemy, and covering the approaches to Washington; while on the ninth the cavalry inflicted a severe blow upon Jeb. Stuart's troopers, who were gathering in strong force at Kelly's Ford, twenty-five miles above Falmouth, intending to sweep with destruction the fertile fields of Pennsylvania.

The Second Corps was the last to leave the line of the Rappahannock. On the eighth of June, the Twenty-seventh Connecticut received orders to be ready to march at any time, with three days' rations, and continued in this waiting posture until the fourteenth instant, when the final orders came, and at three P.M. the regiment, with the rest of the brigade acting as rear-guard to the corps, moved up the river to Banks's Ford, relieved our pickets, reconnoitered the enemy, and retired toward Stafford Court-House. This little hamlet was left behind in flames. For several days the corps followed the roads near the Potomac, passing through Dumfries, Occoquan, and Fairfax Station, halting here two days, and arriving at Centreville on the nineteenth. The route now turned still farther to the left, crossing the old Bull Run battle-field, which had witnessed the decision of two campaigns. Time had not effaced the evidences of those disastrous days. Silently the troops moved over the field, and the thoughts of many a one among the older regiments, and of some in our own, hurried back to those scenes with impressive distinctness, as the bleached bones of the fallen, or the rubbish of battle, lay scattered along the roadside. After a severe march of twenty miles in the rain, the regiment arrived, at ten in the evening of June twentieth, at Thoroughfare Gap, a wild gorge in the Blue Ridge. The intensely exhausting march from Falmouth made the four days of comparative rest at the Gap exceedingly welcome. Here the troops were occupied in picketing the pass, in order to prevent the enemy from crossing the mountains. Meanwhile, to the north, Stuart and Pleasanton were once more on the charge at Aldie, Upperville, and Middleburg, and their muffled cannonade echoed among these hills and pleasant valleys, surely not unused to the sound, repeating itself again and again, as if from as many different directions.

June twenty-fifth, the regiment fell in at an early hour, ready to fight or march, as circumstances might require, for the rebels were approaching with malicious intent to capture the corps' beef cattle and supply train, and sharp picket firing indicated the possible necessity of adopting the former alternative. But after remaining in line of battle, with no serious demonstration on the part of the enemy, the corps advanced through Haymarket, toward the Potomac. The rebel cavalry followed vigorously, and attempted to come in on our flanks, but skirmishers were thrown out, and the troops marched in hollow squares, prepared to repel any attack. At Haymarket, the batteries turned on the enemy, and drove them back. The column pushed forward to Gum Springs, and without pitching tents rested that night on their arms, drawn up in a hollow square, ready at a moment's warning to meet any assault of rebel cavalry. At midnight of June twenty-sixth, the regiment crossed the Potomac at Edward's Ferry. The next three days passed in continuous marching up the valley of the Monocacy river, through many quiet Maryland villages, among them Poolesville, Frederick City, Liberty, Johnsville, and Uniontown. Each day's march was very protracted—that from Frederick City to Uniontown embracing a distance of thirty-six miles, and the manner in which it was performed elicited high compliments from Colonel Brooke, commanding the brigade.

Thus far the army had been manœuvred so as to cover Washington and Baltimore, and now, as the rebel plans became more apparent, General Meade, who had recently superseded General Hooker, directed a concentration of his forces in the vicinity of Gettysburg. The First Corps held the advance, followed by the Eleventh, and on Wednesday morning, July first, drove the enemy's skirmishers through the town. General Reynolds, in command of the corps, without hesitation moved forward to the attack, and met death while bravely posting his troops on the heights beyond. The rebels fell back slowly, in order to give time for Ewell's men to come to their aid, and this being accomplished, they were more than a match for the combined First and Eleventh, with whose now united columns rested the decision of the day. At three in the afternoon, the enemy, thus reënforced, took the offensive, and compelled General Howard, now in command, to withdraw his troops to the south of the town, and the close of the day left him securely intrenched on Cemetery Hill.

While these scenes were taking place around Gettysburg, the Twenty-seventh Connecticut, with its corps, leisurely moved up to Taneytown, just below the Pennsylvania State line. Here the troops rested a few hours, unconscious that the first of a trio of glorious battle days was already in progress. But soon the ominous notes of Howard's and Ewell's cannon strike on the ear, and add new emphasis to the call from the front for reënforcements. Preceded by General Hancock, the corps advanced rapidly to within three miles of Gettysburg, and were occupied until midnight in throwing up intrenchments. At early dawn, July second, the brigades moved forward to take the places assigned them in the line of battle. Already the fitful fire of opposing pickets and skirmishers can be heard in the distance, with the occasional boom of heavy ordnance. The shock of battle, which is to determine the fate of the rebel invasion, will at the farthest be postponed but a few hours. Just before coming into position, and while the troops were resting under arms, the commander of our brigade assembled the officers, and briefly reminded them of the desperate character of the emergency, and urged the importance and necessity of devoting every energy to insure the successful issue of the conflict.

In order to understand the various positions of the Twenty-seventh during the action, let us briefly sketch the line of battle, as adopted by General Hancock, and along which the several corps were arranged, as they arrived on the field. Three important roads, the Emmettsburg, Taneytown, and Baltimore turnpike, converge in Gettysburg from the south. At their junction, just below the town, is the natural key of the position, the now historic Cemetery Hill. This elevation forms the northern end of a ridge prolonged about four miles, almost exactly due south, near to and parallel with the Taneytown road, gradually diminishing in altitude until it almost loses itself in the surrounding level, then rises again into the forest-crowned Little Round Top, or Weed's Hill, and terminates in the yet higher ascent of Rocky Round Top itself. Beginning on the left at Round Top, the Union line extends northward in nearly a straight course along Cemetery Ridge, and at Cemetery Hill bends back to the east in the general form of a half circle, with a radius of three fourths of a mile—Culp's Hill, and several minor eminences, lying in the circumference; and the extreme right, crossing Rock Creek, which flows at the base of these heights, rests upon the woody summit of Wolf's Hill. The rebel forces occupied a series of heights corresponding to these, with an intervening belt of comparatively level and open country from one to two miles in width.

The forenoon of Thursday, July second, passed with no demonstration on either side. The hostile forces are rapidly marshalling on the opposite ridges. In the Union line the Twelfth Corps holds the eminences near Rock Creek, on the right; next is the First, on Culp's Hill; then the Eleventh, at the centre, on Cemetery Hill, while along Cemetery Ridge are successively drawn up the Second, Third, and Fifth, with the Sixth in reserve near the Taneytown road. The Twenty-seventh Connecticut was stationed about a mile and a half south of Cemetery Hill, in the line occupied by our Second Corps on the left centre. Here the regiment remained nearly all day in quiet preparation for the conflict, which threatened at any moment to mar that peaceful landscape of thrifty farm-houses and waving grain.

Early in the afternoon, the Third Corps, on the left of the Second, advanced down the western slope of Cemetery Ridge, through woods and an extensive wheat-field, almost to the Emmettsburg road, which winds through the narrow valley, separating the hostile forces. Just beyond, Longstreet is forming his brigades, and at four o'clock, preceded by a brief cannonade, their gray ranks sweep out from woods and ravines, and once more is heard that strange, wild yell, as they throw themselves forward upon the thin line of the Third Corps. But before the storm of grape and canister from Cemetery Ridge they quickly fall back to organize anew their broken columns. Meanwhile reënforcements from the Fifth and Second Corps moved rapidly to the scene of action. Once more in still heavier masses the enemy advanced to the charge. The Twenty-seventh, with the rest of the First Division, was hurried forward through fields and by-roads, to support the faltering line. As the regiment enters the wheat-field, already referred to, the broken remains of the Third Corps are slowly retiring to the rear. A few steps more bring the men under the full sweep of the enemy's fire. Lieutenant-Colonel Merwin falls while leading the command with his accustomed bravery. Under Major Coburn, the line still presses forward at double-quick, through the wheat-field and woods beyond, driving the rebels a quarter of a mile, across a ravine, which on the further side rises into a precipitous ledge. The men with much difficulty clambered up the rocky steep, but as they appeared upon the crest of the hill, the enemy, drawn up in readiness just beyond, within pistol-range, opened upon them a withering fire. The contest at this point continued for some time. Planting the colors upon the top, the men loaded their pieces under shelter of the brow of the hill, then, rising up, delivered their fire. Meanwhile the troops to our right gave way, and, taking advantage of the exposed position of the right flank of our brigade, the enemy advanced a body of troops in that direction, and General Brooke at length ordered our shattered line to fall back, which was accomplished under a heavy cross-fire.

Thus with varying success the battle raged from four P.M. until dark. Now the feeble line of the Third Corps trembles before the fierce onset of the foe, and retires, contesting the ground inch by inch; but the irresistible onslaught of reënforcements soon turns the tide. Again the rebels push back the Union troops almost to the original lines on Cemetery Ridge, and again are themselves repulsed before the concentrated fire of our artillery, aiding the charge of a brigade of infantry.

The conflict on the left wing terminated at dark, leaving the enemy in possession of the wheat-field. No attack had yet been made upon other parts of the line, but, as the day closed, a division, deploying from the edge of the town, made a brief and desperate, but fruitless, assault upon the batteries posted on Cemetery Hill. And still further to the right, the enemy, observing that the larger part of the forces on Culp's Hill had been drawn off to meet pressing emergencies elsewhere, crossed Rock Creek, and, charging up the woody slope, secured a lodgement for the night in the unoccupied portion of the works. Such was the general result of the day's fighting.

The Twenty-seventh went into action with seventy-five men, all that could be mustered for duty after an active service of not quite nine months. At the camps of paroled prisoners, the Richmond voyagers of our regiment, though not permitted to rejoin the command, yet in thought followed their comrades through all the vicissitudes of march and battle which attended them. At five P.M. that little band of seventy-five men formed for the charge at the edge of the wheat-field. At dark thirty-eight were numbered among the casualties: eleven killed—among them Lieutenant-Colonel Merwin, and Captain Jedediah Chapman—twenty-three wounded, and four missing. One of the latter, when Lee's army retreated, was marched by his captors from Gettysburg to Staunton, Virginia, one hundred and eighty miles, and thence transported by railroad to Richmond. After a six weeks' experience on Belle Island, he was paroled, and returned home so emaciated and worn down by hardship as to be almost beyond recognition even by members of his own company.

At the close of the action in front of the left wing, the Twenty-seventh was assigned a new position in the line of battle, about midway on the ridge between Cemetery Hill and Round Top. The regiment remained in this vicinity until the Second Corps started in pursuit of Lee's army, three days later. Early the next morning, July third, the men were roused from sleep by a furious cannonade from batteries posted on Power's Hill, about half a mile to the rear. These dogs of war were paying their morning compliments to the rebels, who still occupied the works on the extreme right, which they had captured the previous evening. For an hour this thunder-toned reveille awoke the resting armies to the still fiercer drama of the last battle day. The infantry followed up this fiery prelude with a vigorous attack upon the rebel vantage-ground, the importance of which seemed fully appreciated by both sides. The struggle continued with unabated resolution until nine o'clock, when the Union forces succeeded in dispossessing the enemy of this to them valuable *point d'appui* for future operations.

With the exception of a severe artillery fire, to which General Meade's headquarters were subjected, the enemy attempted nothing further during the remainder of the forenoon. The Twenty-seventh was busily engaged in throwing up intrenchments, gathering for this purpose rails and stones from neighboring fences, and, in the absence of picks and shovels, using their bayonets and tin plates to heap up the earth. In his morning rounds, General Hancock visited the brigade, and as he stood near by, conversing with Major Coburn, our acting Brigadier, Colonel Brooke, called the General's attention to the little remnant of the Twenty-seventh, alluding, in strong terms of commendation, to the conduct of the regiment in the action of the preceding afternoon. Turning to the men, General Hancock said: "Stand well to your duty now, and in a few days you will carry with you to your homes all the honors of this, the greatest battle ever fought upon the continent."

From eleven o'clock until one, only stifled mutterings of the impatient storm disturbed the quiet which reigned along the lines. The rebels were silently maturing their plans for the last grand charge, upon which they staked the fate of the invasion. Those were hours of indescribable suspense to the defenders of the Union, whether or no the sun would set upon a foe elated with victory and pressing onward to new conquests, or sullenly retiring in defeat. At one o'clock the combat began. From every commanding eminence in their concave line, the rebel artillery, numbering more than a hundred guns, opened a terrific cannonade, probably unsurpassed in violence during the whole war. For more than an hour this wild storm of shot and shell rolls over the Union line, from Round Top to Rock Creek. The infantry are partially sheltered behind intrenchments, while the cannoneers stand at their posts, replying occasionally to the bombardment, but reserving their fire for more decisive work, when the rebel forces advance to the assault. At length the cannonade slackens, to give way to the next act in the drama, the crisis of the tragedy. In full view two heavy lines of troops, the flower of the rebel army, with skirmishers in front, deploy from the woods and ridges beyond the Emmettsburg road. With the steadiness of hardened veterans they move forward to the attack. From Cemetery Ridge thousands of Union troops are watching their progress, for the assault is directed upon the left centre. On arriving at the road, the enemy opened a heavy musketry fire, and dashed rapidly forward across the level plain. The very moment they emerged from behind Seminary Heights, the Union artillery met them with shot and shell and solid shot, but now, as they approach within easy range, their ranks are mercilessly raked with a tempest of canister. Cemetery Hill is wreathed with flame from the guns of thickly-massed infantry, and the fringe of fire courses along the crest of the ridge for two miles, as far as the rebel attack extends. Though temporarily checked, one division still marches on with desperate energy up to the very works. Only a weak line bars their progress, but reinforcements quickly arrive at the critical point, around which the contending hosts now struggle, in one of the most hotly-contested encounters of the battle. For a time the rebels bravely maintain their position, but clouds of missiles from Cemetery Hill tear into their ranks, while infantry crowd them vigorously in front and flank. At length, leaving the ground thickly strewn with killed and wounded, and multitudes as prisoners in the hands of the conquerors, the broken remnants roll back in wild confusion, and disappear behind the hills from which they had sallied forth.

This last charge of the rebels took place just to the right of the position held by the Twenty-seventh, which we have already referred to as being half-way between Round Top and Cemetery Hill. From the relation of the ground to the surrounding high land, the location of our brigade was regarded as one of the weakest in the line, and General Hancock expressed the opinion that here the enemy would make his attack. Fortunately it proved otherwise, although for a time such a movement seemed imminent. Near the close of the action, a division, massed in column, advanced directly upon our front, but the reserve artillery quickly drove them back before they came within musketry range. The favorable termination of what was felt to be the last assault the rebels would make, produced a profound feeling of satisfaction. But one of the saddest of duties remained to be performed—to bury the dead and gather the wounded into the hospitals. This work occupied the men during July fourth. On that day, Lee's army withdrew from this scene of inglorious defeat, and retired in a southwesterly direction.

In the afternoon of July fifth, the war-worn Twenty-seventh, with the Second Corps, left those battle-scarred heights, the theatre of a costly but substantial triumph, which marks the turning-point in the fortunes of the rebellion. For the next few days the march was directed toward the Potomac, following at first the Taneytown road. But slow progress was made, in consequence of frequent rains and the thoroughly exhausted condition of the troops. The state of popular feeling along the route was in striking contrast with the dejected aspect of every countenance when the army was on its way to Gettysburg. Now, Frederick City put on its most smiling face. Flags were flung to the breeze, and the people gave an enthusiastic welcome to the regiments as they passed through in pursuit of Lee's army. The route now crossed the Blue Ridge, by way of Crampton's Gap. Here the severe rains had gathered a considerable torrent, several feet deep, which formed the pathway of the troops for nearly two miles. The Twenty-seventh was once more in the vicinity of the enemy, who had retreated down the western slope of the mountains, and were now in position at Williamsport, on the Potomac, preparing to cross into Virginia. The sound of cannon in that direction informed us that they were but a short distance to the front; and while on the field of Antietam, the brigade formed in line of battle, as a precautionary measure. The next day the rebel cavalry attacked the skirmish line, but quickly fell back before a severe shelling. In anticipation of further fighting, the men spent two nights and one day in building an elaborate line of intrenchments; but it proved to be labor lost, as the rebels retired, on the night of the fourteenth, to the south bank of the river. Immediately on ascertaining this fact, the Twenty-seventh, with the brigade, was ordered down to Falling Waters, a short distance below Williamsport, and arrived there just in time to witness the capture of the enemy's rear-guard, more than a thousand strong.

The invasion was now at an end; and as the last rebel left the soil of Maryland, the campaign of the Twenty-seventh drew near to its close. Leaving Falling Waters, the regiment accompanied the Second Corps down the Potomac to Harper's Ferry, and went into camp at Pleasant Valley, about two miles distant. On the morning of July eighteenth the Twenty-seventh ceased its connection with the Army of the Potomac. In announcing this event, Colonel Brooke, our brigade commander, issued the following general order:

"HEADQUARTERS FOURTH BRIGADE, FIRST DIVISION, }
SECOND CORPS, CAMP IN PLEASANT VALLEY, }
MARYLAND, July 17, 1863. }

"GENERAL ORDER—NO. 9.

"The term of service of the Twenty-seventh Connecticut Volunteers having nearly expired, it has been relieved from further duty, and ordered to report to its place of enrolment.

"The Colonel commanding the brigade desires, in parting with the officers and men of the Twenty-seventh Connecticut, to convey to them his sincere feelings of regret at losing their services, while at the same time he thanks them for the obedience and faithfulness which have been a marked feature of the regiment.

"Knowing it intimately for so many months of active and arduous service—having been an eye-witness of its many deeds of gallantry, and of the noble devotion displayed by it on many a memorable day, during the time in which he has had the honor to command its services—he feels it a duty he owes, not only to the living heroes, but to the memory of those who have fallen in the field in battling in our righteous cause, to bear testimony to the valor and gallantry it has always displayed.

"Side by side with the veterans of the Army of the Potomac it has fought, and by the gallantry of its conduct won for itself an enviable name and reputation, and which may well, in after years, cause all who belong to it to feel a pardonable pride in having it to say that they served with the Twenty-seventh Connecticut.

"By order. COLONEL BROOKE.

"CHARLES P. HATCH, Lieutenant,
"Acting Assistant Adjutant-General."

With glad hearts the men formed in line at an early hour and took the cars for Baltimore, after a parting salute to the brigade, as it marched by on its way into Virginia. On the twentieth, the detachments of paroled men from Annapolis and Camp Convalescent arrived at Baltimore, and the whole regiment, now mustering about half the original number, started by railroad for New-Haven. Once more we were entertained at the "Volunteer Refreshment Saloon," in Philadelphia, and, after a night's bivouack at the Battery, in New-York, arrived at the "place of enrolment" on the twenty-second of July, 1863, exactly nine months from the date of departure for the field. We shall not attempt to describe the hearty enthusiasm and deep feeling of the reception which followed. That "glorious welcome home" will long be remembered by the soldiers of the Twenty-seventh. Escorted by the military companies of the city and the municipal authorities, the regiment marched from the cars to the north portico of the State House, while "Welcome!" pealed from the ringing bells, thundered in the roar of cannon, waved from every flag-staff, and shone on every countenance of the vast multitude, gathered from all parts of the county, and thronging the streets and public square. At the State House, after the regiment had been drawn up "in column by division," the Mayor presented the formal welcome of the city, and was succeeded by Rev. Dr. Bacon in a brief address, closing with a prayer of thanksgiving. The following poem, written by Mrs. William Doty, of New-Haven, and accompanying a gift of laurel wreaths to the field-officers, was then read:

A TRIBUTE OF WELCOME

TO THE TWENTY-SEVENTH CONNECTICUT VOLUNTEERS.

We'll fling to the breeze our banner bright,

America's emblem of freedom and right,

And rallying round the standard true,

Shout a joyous welcome, brave patriots, to you.

Ye went forth from us, a loyal band,
Firm on the side of right to stand;
Ye return with hearts still brave and true;
Then our warmest greeting we give to you.

Ye return, but our tears will fall as ye come,
For the mournful notes of the muffled drum
Are borne on the breeze over mountain and wave,
As it beats the dirge by your comrades' grave.

With the order, "Forward!" ye marched proudly on,
And your colors bright to the front were borne;
When the smoke of the battle had cleared away,
Side by side with the "veterans" your brave boys lay.

Through the summer's heat and winter's cold
At your post ye stood, fearless and bold;
And when on the field, 'mid the conflict dire,
Ye *did not* "quail at the enemy's fire."

Oh! the road to Richmond hath altars bright,
Where, a "captive band," ye camped at night,
And "Libby's" grim walls a record bears,
Of the patriot's song and the hero's prayers.

Now the toil is over, the march is done;
And the wreath of laurel, ye've bravely won,
We offer to you, and our welcome it breathes,
For our prayers were twined with its glossy leaves.

But ye're not *all* here, and we'll look in vain
For the smiles that will greet us never again;
And the quivering lip and tearful eye

Mutely ask you where our treasures lie.

Some sleep where Virginia's waters flow,
Murmuring their requiem soft and low;
Others with fairest flowers were drest,
And close by the old homes laid to rest.

When the angel of peace, with brooding wing,
Shall fly o'er our land and its anthem sing,
With trembling fingers the strings she'll sweep,
As she nears the spot where our loved ones sleep.

Then a costly crown will our country wear,
And bright the gems that shall sparkle there.
She shall sit a queen, peerless and free,
And the graves of her heroes her glory be!

Still firmly stand, in God your trust,
Till the rebel horde shall bite the dust,
And the North and South encircled be
With the bands of truth and liberty.

Fight on, till our starry flag of blue,
Each glistening fold to its purpose true,
Shall wave from wild Atlantic's roar
To the golden strands of Pacific's shore.

At the conclusion of these exercises a bountiful collation was served up, after which the men separated, to await the completion of the papers necessary to the final muster out of service, which took place July twenty-seventh, 1863.

Thus terminated the eventful campaign of the Twenty-seventh Connecticut Volunteers. During this brief term of nine months, the regiment performed marches in Virginia, Maryland, and Pennsylvania, amounting to no less than five hundred miles, and participated in three of the great battles of the war—

Fredericksburg, Chancellorsville, and Gettysburg—losing in killed and wounded in the first, about one third, and in the last, one half, of those present in action. Very many of our number, on their return, reënlisted in other organizations, and illustrated on new fields the same valor which bore them and their comrades up the fiery slope of Fredericksburg, nerved all hearts calmly to meet disaster in the wilderness of Chancellorsville, and crowned with victory the heights of Gettysburg.

IN MEMORIAM.

The necrology of the Twenty-seventh, during the whole term of service, includes seventy-five officers and men, and embraces much that was noblest in the regiment. Of this number thirty-three fell amid the strife and turmoil of battle; eighteen, after a more or less lingering period of patient agony, finally succumbed to their wounds; and twenty-four others slowly yielded to the inroads of disease, and died among the more quiet scenes of the hospital. Were it possible, we would gladly dwell upon each individual name, and gather up those qualities by which each is remembered among his comrades. But after all that might be said, the simple record of the central fact in their history, that these men fell in defence of the most righteous cause ever submitted to the decision of the sword, is far more impressive than any commemorative words. And yet there are some whose marked character and prominent connection with the regiment as a whole, or with single companies, seem to demand more than a passing notice. Chief among these, the mind and heart of each member of the regiment will at once recur to the name of

LIEUT.-COL. HENRY C. MERWIN,

who fell in the battle of Gettysburg, July second, 1863. If this noble spirit must leave its mortal tenement amid the wild tumult of war, how appropriate that it should be when the black cloud of disaster, which had so long hovered over the cause of our country, was just rolling away, and already revealed its silver lining of victory!

Colonel Merwin was a native of Brookfield, Connecticut, where he was born September seventeenth, 1839. He spent the greater part of his life in New-Haven, and at the beginning of the war was in business with his father and brother. He early manifested a fondness for military life, to which the subsequent events of his history proved him well adapted. When the first gun of the war sounded from the rebel batteries at Charleston, it awoke in his breast a determined and prompt response. At that time he was a member of the New-Haven Grays, and immediately volunteered with that corps for three months' service in the Second Regiment, holding the position of sergeant. It will be remembered that that was one of the very few regiments which returned with credit from the field of Bull Run. After this brief campaign he remained at home for a season, constrained by considerations of filial duty, by which a noble nature like his is ever governed until yet higher obligations demand attention. The armies of the Union were being rapidly filled up, and at length the Government stopped recruiting, while the nation beheld with confidence the vast and apparently irresistible preparations, which betokened an easy victory. Under these circumstances it was not strange that so many, like Colonel Merwin, held back by peculiar home duties, refrained from throwing themselves into the struggle. But these anticipations resulted in disappointment, and all this array of resources proved a disastrous failure. The call of the country was now heard in louder and more imperative tones than ever before, and appealed to a far wider circle in the community. Henry C. Merwin responded with a calm, but earnest alacrity, as is ever true of those whose guide is duty. His deserved and unsought popularity soon gathered to his banner a full quota of men, which was designated as Company A of the Twenty-seventh. Subsequently, at the organization of the regiment, he was chosen Lieutenant-Colonel by the votes of his fellow-officers. From this point his history is identified with that of the regiment. From the moment of departure for the field to the time of his death in that terrible combat of July second, at Gettysburg, he had never been relieved from duty, except as the casualties of war separated him from his command. He shared the fortunes of the regiment during the terrible and fruitless battle of Fredericksburg, and met with undaunted courage the sudden shock of disaster in the thickets of Chancellorsville. He visited Richmond as a prisoner of war, and on being exchanged at once returned to the regiment, to the command of which he was now called. Along the weary march to Gettysburg he inspired the men with his own indomitable spirit, and on that fated wheat-field, where the missiles of the enemy, as it were, mowed down the waving grain, he fell, mortally wounded, breathing out those words of noble self-forgetfulness, "My poor regiment is suffering fearfully."

Without disparagement to any, it may truly be said that no officer in the regiment attracted to himself such universal and unvarying respect, confidence, and affection among the men of his command. Nor was this strange in view of the remarkable and harmonious combination of noble qualities in his character. No pride of position ever marred the beautiful consistency of his life, and yet there was a natural dignity which forbade undue familiarity. He felt deeply the responsibility of his relation to the regiment, and this o'ermastering principle swallowed up every consideration of self-interest. Duty was evidently the supreme motive of his life, and intent upon the performance of his own, he expected and required equal faithfulness on the part of others. He was quick of discernment, and rapid in execution, but no harshness ever dimmed the transparent kindness of his demeanor. His genial countenance and words of sympathy and encouragement often cheered the loneliness of the hospital. He thoroughly appreciated the hardships and trials peculiar to the private soldier, and at all times endeavored to sustain and inspirit his weary energies. All these more amiable qualities were supplemented by a manly independence and decision, which made him always jealous for the rights of his men. On that trying march to Gettysburg, no arrogance and severity of superior officers ever deterred him from a gentlemanly, but bold and firm, maintenance of the rights and interests of the regiment. He at once secured the respect, and soon the high regard of Colonel Brooke, commanding the brigade, who felt most keenly the loss of Colonel Merwin, and, on hearing that he was wounded, gave orders that every thing possible should be done for his welfare.

But none can do justice to such a character. In his death the Twenty-seventh laid its costliest sacrifice upon the altar of our country.

"He had kept

The brightness of his soul, and thus men o'er him wept."

ADDISON C. TAYLOR,

Captain of Company C.

This gallant officer fell severely wounded in the engagement at Fredericksburg, December thirteenth, 1862, and died at his home in New-Haven, March thirteenth, 1863. He was born October twenty-eighth, 1841, in Wellington, Lorraine county, Ohio. His parents were natives of Connecticut, which State became his home when he was about twelve years of age. For several years he was a pupil in the Collegiate and Commercial Institute of New-Haven, and subsequently a teacher, and also the military instructor in that school. The outbreak of the rebellion in 1861 found him performing the duties of this position. Though feeling that his relations and duties to others did not permit him at that time to enter the active military service of the country, yet he took an earnest and enthusiastic part in the stirring scenes of that period. Troops were to be raised and prepared for the field with the utmost dispatch. How vividly memory recalls the experiences of those days, then so strange in our national history, when men were gathering from all quarters for the nation's defence, and our streets resounded with the drum and fife, and the public square was alive with squads and companies moving to and fro in the mazes of military evolutions! Captain Taylor's zeal and military knowledge found an ample sphere for exercise at this important crisis, and truly most efficient service did he render. It should be particularly mentioned, that he drilled the company of Captain, now Brevet Major-General, Joseph R. Hawley, then of the First Connecticut Regiment of three months' volunteers. Brevet Brigadier-General Edward W. Whittaker, the adventurous cavalry leader, was also at that time a member of this company. So successfully did Captain Taylor fulfil these duties that Captain Hawley offered him the most flattering inducements if he would consent to accompany the regiment; but the time had not arrived when he was to give even life itself for his country. It came when the battle summer of 1862 convinced the nation that this was no ordinary struggle, and brought each man face to face with the question of his own individual duty. At this juncture the call was issued for volunteers for nine months' service; and Captain Taylor, with his accustomed ardor, immediately entered upon the work of recruiting the "Monitors" for the Twenty-seventh Regiment, and soon assembled about him a very superior body of men, to whom his military knowledge and experience were of very great advantage. His was the color company, and at its head he moved on that day of fearful carnage, the memorable thirteenth of December, 1862, when he received the wound which resulted in death, after three months of patient suffering.

Did space allow, we might appropriately introduce at this point the singularly unanimous testimony of those who knew him best, to the self-reliance which he manifested from his earliest years; to the thorough, unostentatious sincerity, purity, and conscientiousness of his life; to the high sense of duty which impelled him to the field, and animated him in every act; and, more than all this, to the Christian principles which formed the basis of his symmetrical character.

"The light of his young life went down,

As sinks behind the hill

The glory of a setting star—

Clear, suddenly, and still.

The blessing of his quiet life

Was in his every look.

We read his face as one that reads

A true and holy book."

JEDEDIAH CHAPMAN, Jr.,

CAPTAIN OF COMPANY H.

Death singled out another shining mark when Captain Chapman fell in the fore-front of battle, on the same afternoon that beheld the close of Colonel Merwin's life. Two congenial spirits in nobility and worth together passed to the land of immortality on that day of death's high carnival.

Jedediah Chapman, Jr., was born in New-Haven, November twenty-first, 1839. Like Colonel Merwin, he was a member of the New-Haven Grays at the opening of the war, and accompanied them to the field as a private in the three months' service. When the Twenty-seventh was being recruited under the call for nine months' troops, he took hold of the work with vigor, and was in great part instrumental in raising Company H, of which he was chosen First Lieutenant. During more than one third of the campaign he had command of the company, and to his exertions and military experience its efficiency was largely due. Amid the terrors of that disastrous day at Fredericksburg, no one acquitted himself with greater bravery and coolness than Lieutenant Chapman. In consequence of protracted sickness during the spring of 1863, he did not participate in the battle of Chancellorsville, and thus escaped the fate of the regiment. But it was a great disappointment to him not to be with his men, and share with them the vicissitudes of the campaign. By reason of the disaster to the Twenty-seventh in that battle, only two companies of the regiment remained in the field, with a few remnants of those which were captured. These scattering portions were formed into one company, and Lieutenant Chapman was placed in command. His peculiar qualifications of discipline and character contributed much to their unity and effectiveness during the succeeding campaign of Gettysburg; and at their head he fell on the second of July, 1863. His commission as Captain of Company H, dated May thirteenth, 1863, had been already issued and forwarded; but he did not live to know of this well-deserved honor.

Much that has already been said of Colonel Merwin might, with equal propriety, be applied to Captain Chapman. He was an officer well known, and highly esteemed, not only in his own company, but throughout the regiment. He possessed in a peculiar degree all the elements which constitute an efficient, and yet popular, commander. In all his relations, he manifested a genial frankness of manner, a conscientiousness of purpose, and keen sense of justice, which at once gained universal confidence and regard. He was one of the most unassuming of men, and yet in that soul burned a depth of devotion to duty, and a power of noble action, which seemed to require the stern, trying scenes of war to bring them forth in their original strength and glory. So long as the campaign of the Twenty-seventh lives in the memory of those who participated in it, so long will the members of Company H cherish the name and reputation of their beloved commander, Jedediah Chapman.

Let us now turn to the long catalogue of enlisted men, whose names appear in the necrology of the regiment. History can never do justice to the grandeur and far-reaching importance of the cause to which they gave the testimony of their lives, nor can it do justice to the nobility and value of the sacrifice. It is not necessary to repeat in this place the names of these worthy men; but we will call to mind a few representatives of their number. There was Orderly-Sergeant Richard H. Fowler, of Company A, who died of wounds received at Fredericksburg. He was a native of Guilford, and one of a family whose record for active patriotism and sublimity of sacrifice has few, if any, parallels during the whole war. Corporal William A. Goodwin and Private Augustus B. Fairchild likewise fell at Fredericksburg. To the efficiency and worth of them all, the officers of the company bear willing testimony. Companies C, D, E, and F, also suffered severely in the loss of faithful and tried soldiers. The battle of Fredericksburg struck from the roll of Company H some of its most valued members. Among these were Orderly-Sergeant Thomas E. Barrett, and Corporals George H. Mimmac and Frank E. Ailing. Sergeant Barrett was a man of very superior character and education. Previous to his enlistment he had been a much-esteemed teacher at the Eaton Public School in New-Haven. The pleasant duties and associations of this position, and all its prospects of usefulness, he yielded up to enter the service of the country. Few made greater sacrifices, or made them more cheerfully, than he, in obedience to a purely unselfish sense of duty. He sought and expected no office, and only at the earnest solicitation of his comrades consented to accept the post of First Sergeant, and certainly no company ever had a more faithful and conscientious officer. He was a noble Christian soldier; a man whom society could ill afford to lose. But he has left behind him an example which should be carefully cherished and regarded. The sacrifice of such a man is of no ordinary value, and gives unusual significance to the struggle through which the nation has passed. Corporals Mimmac and Ailing possessed very similar elements of character. The latter was a member of Yale College at the time he enlisted, and left the congenial pursuits of a student's life to respond to what he regarded the call of duty. Such were some of the men the ranks of the Twenty-seventh contributed to that roll of honored names, whose heroism and self-sacrifice will grow brighter and brighter, as the progress of years reveals, in all their meaning and influence, the events of the war for Liberty and Union.

RECORD OF CASUALTIES.

FIELD AND STAFF.

KILLED.

At Gettysburg, July 2, 1863.

Lieutenant-Colonel Henry C. Merwin.

WOUNDED.

At Fredericksburg, December 13, 1862.

Chaplain John W. Leek.

At Gettysburg.

Adjutant George F. Peterson.

COMPANY A.

KILLED.

At Fredericksburg.

Corporal William A. Goodwin, Jr.

Private Augustus B. Fairchild.

WOUNDED.

At Fredericksburg.

First Sergeant Richard H. Fowler.

Sergeant Nelson S. Wilmot.

Sergeant James B. Blair.

Corporal William H. Cornwall.

Private Thomas H. Wallace.

DIED OF WOUNDS.

First Sergeant Richard H. Fowler, December 17th, 1862, at camp near Falmouth.

DIED OF DISEASE.

Private Henry B. Hilliard, December 17th, 1862, at Hammond General Hospital, Maryland.

Private Edward C. Hazard, October 16th, 1862, at Camp Terry, New-Haven.

Private Frank A. Johnson, December 14th, 1862, at camp near Falmouth.

Private Treat A. Marks, December 25th, 1862, at camp near Falmouth.

Private Joseph B. Thompson, February 7th, 1863, at camp near Falmouth.

Private Elbert W. Ball, August 5th, 1863, at New-Haven.

COMPANY B.
WOUNDED.

At Fredericksburg..

Corporal George E. Wilford.

Private Timothy Callahan.

Private Joseph Bennett.

Patrick Condon.

Josiah Johnson.

Michael Taylor.

L. Mortimer Willis.

Edwin L. Wilford.

At Gettysburg.

Private Charles Paxden.

DIED OF WOUNDS.

Corporal George E. Wilford, January 8th, 1863.

Private Joseph Bennett, December 25th, 1862.

Patrick Condon, December 28th, 1862, in hospital at Annapolis.

Josiah Johnson, January 5th, 1863.

DIED OF DISEASE.

Private George C. Baldwin, January 25th, 1863, at camp near Falmouth.

Private Edward B. Dolph, March 20th, 1863, at camp near Falmouth.

Private Lewis M. Tucker, October 10th, 1862, at Branford, Connecticut.
Second Lieutenant Edmund B. Cross, August 6th, 1863, at New-Haven.

COMPANY C.
KILLED.

At Fredericksburg.

Private Charles Michael.
Wilbur Nash.
Joel C. Parmelee.

At Chancellorsville.

Private Samuel B. Clark.

At Gettysburg.

Corporal Charles E. Cornwall.
Color-Corporal Joseph Stevens.

WOUNDED.

At Fredericksburg.

Captain Addison C. Taylor.
Second Lieutenant Charles B. Brooks.
Sergeant Henry M. Stanton.
Color-Corporal Henry E. Wing.
Color-Corporal James L. Ambler.
Color-Corporal Sydney R. Thompson.
Private Hector Murphy.
John Platt.
George W. Hine.

At Chancellorsville.

Sergeant Charles S. Beatty.

At Gettysburg.

Color-Corporal William S. Bodwell.

Corporal Gilbert A. W. Ford.

DIED OF WOUNDS.

Captain Addison C. Taylor, March 13th, 1863, at New-Haven, Connecticut.

Color-Corporal William L. Bodwell, July 5th, 1863, at Gettysburg.

Color-Corporal Sydney R. Thompson, December 30th, 1862.

DIED OF DISEASE.

Color-Corporal Sydney H. Plumb, April 18th, 1863, at camp near Falmouth.

Private John G. Clark, December 30th, 1862, in General Hospital, Washington.

Private Harvey S. Welton, July 14th, 1863, near Harper's Ferry, Virginia.

COMPANY D.

KILLED.

At Fredericksburg.

Sergeant Garry B. Sperry.

Private William Reuter.

Gilbert Keller.

At Gettysburg.

Private William O. Scott.

William E. Wilson.

Patrick Dunn.

Marcus O. Judson.

John Goodwin.

WOUNDED.

At Fredericksburg.

First Lieutenant Frank H. Smith.

Second Lieutenant Ellsworth A. Smith.

Sergeant John A. Munson.

Henry B. Hill.

Benjamin H. Cobb.

George B. Lego.

Corporal Andrew J. Barnard.

Private James Johnson.

Alpheus D. Cobb.

Thomas M. Kilcullen.

Loren M. Higgins.

John Mitchell.

At Chancellorsville.

Sergeant Fitch M. Parker.

At Gettysburg.

Captain Cornelius J. Dubois.

First Sergeant George T. Swank.

Private Dwight T. Brockett.

Thomas M. Kilcullen.

William Lee.

Charles H. Nichols.

John Phillips.

Richard A. Tenner.

John E. Williamson.

John Hogan.

Thomas G. Yale.

DIED OF WOUNDS.

Sergeant Henry B. Hill, January 14th, 1863.

Benjamin H. Cobb, January 19th, 1863.

Private Loren M. Higgins, February 1st, 1863.

John Mitchell, December 15th, 1862.

Thomas G. Yale, August 26th, 1863, Philadelphia.

DIED OF DISEASE.

Private John W. Lounsbury, December 8th, 1862.

Private William Goodwill, December 10th, 1862, at College Hospital, Georgetown, D. C.

Spencer Bronson.

Thomas M. Kilcullen, September 10th, 1863, in Richmond, Virginia.

COMPANY E.
KILLED.
At Fredericksburg.

Corporal James G. Clinton.

Private George Brown.

Andrew B. Castle.

Edward Thompson.

At Chancellorsville.

Private William Burke.

WOUNDED.

At Fredericksburg.

Sergeant John D. Sherwood.

Private Timothy Carroll.

Seth Woodward.

At Chancellorsville.

Corporal Frederick G. Bell.

Private Edward A. Dunning.

David S. Rockwell.

At Gettysburg.

Private Charles H. Henderson.

DIED OF DISEASE.

Private Jacob Schneider, January 19th, 1863, at camp near Falmouth.

COMPANY F.

KILLED.

At Gettysburg.

Private Michael Confrey.

Edward B. Farr.

WOUNDED.

At Fredericksburg.

First Lieutenant DeWitt C. Sprague.

Sergeant Henry D. Russell.

Corporal Thomas Ward.

James B. Munson.

Elias C. Mix, Jr.

Private John Crosby.

John A. Hopkins.

Charles Higgins.

William A. Kelley.

Dennis W. Tucker.

James Williamson.

Henry C. Wakelee.

Henry A. Kelsey.

Leonard Russell.

William F. Tuttle.

Jairus C. Eddy.

Samuel Fowler, 2d.

At Chancellorsville.

Sergeant Thomas Ward.

Private William Blakeslee.

John Crosby.

At Gettysburg.

Captain Joseph R. Bradley.

First Lieutenant Charles P. Prince.

Sergeant Thomas Ward.

Corporal Henry W. Clark.

Private Edward B. Fowler.

Daniel O'Neal.

DIED OF WOUNDS.

At Fredericksburg.

Sergeant Henry D. Russell, January 4th, 1863, in hospital, Washington.

Private Jairus C. Eddy, December 20th, at camp near Falmouth.

Private Samuel Fowler, 2d, January 9th, in hospital, Washington.

DIED OF DISEASE.

Private John S. Robinson, June 18th, 1863, in Baltimore.

COMPANY G.

WOUNDED.

At Fredericksburg.

Sergeant Casper S. Gladwin.

Corporal Andrew J. Boardman, Jr.

Private Hosea B. Button.

Henry H. Onthrup.

At Gettysburg.

Corporal William H. Stannis.

Private John Griffin.

Martin Merrill.

DIED OF DISEASE.

Nelson N. Beecher, June 24th, 1863.

COMPANY H.

KILLED.

At Fredericksburg.

First Sergeant Thomas E. Barrett.

Corporal Frank E. Alling.

George I. Judson.

George H. Mimmac.

At Chancellorsville.

Private John Rawson.

At Gettysburg.

Captain Jedediah Chapman.

WOUNDED.

At Fredericksburg.

Sergeant Wareham A. Morse.

Frederick E. Munson.

William H. Alden.

Private Joseph A. Rogers.

Leicester J. Sawyer.

Private Hezekiah P. Smith.

Byron Ure.

Frank L. Merwin.

At Chancellorsville.

Private Silas Benham.

James Braddock.

DIED OF DISEASE.

Private Charles L. Alling, March 22d, 1863, at camp near Falmouth.

Private Hezekiah P. Smith, January 18th, 1863, at camp near Falmouth.

COMPANY I.

KILLED.

At Fredericksburg.

Corporal Corydon N. Thomas.

WOUNDED.

At Fredericksburg.

First Lieutenant Samuel M. Smith.

Color-Sergeant James Brand.

Corporal Henry B. Wilcox.

William G. Hill.

Judson H. Dowd.

Private Francis E. Beach.

Dennis Crummy.

Henry D. Calkins.

Alvah R. Doane.

Samuel J. Field.

Private George S. Hill.

Thomas Pentelow.

Julian F. Watrous.

At Chancellorsville.

Private George W. Beckwith.

DIED OF WOUNDS.

Corporal William G. Hill, January 6th, 1863, in Washington.

Private Rufus S. Shelley, December 29th, 1862, in hospital, at Georgetown, D. C.

DIED OF DISEASE.

Private Joseph Hull, March 2d, 1863, at camp near Falmouth.

Private George S. Hill.

William M. Phile, April 20th, 1863.

COMPANY K.

KILLED.

At Fredericksburg.

Captain Bernard E. Schweizer.

Corporal Albert Cabanis.

WOUNDED.

At Fredericksburg.

Corporal Augustus Vogt.

Private John Huber.

George Gunther.

Ernst Klein.

Ernst Reuthe.

John Schaffner.

At Chancellorsville.

Private Michael Hauserman.

George Eckle.

DIED OF DISEASE.

Private William F. Bernhardt, June 15th, 1863.

Tabular Statement of Casualties during the Nine Months' Campaign.

Legend:–
F: Fredericksburg.
C: Chancellorsville.
G: Gettysburg.
D: Of Disease.
WF: Of wounds rec'd at Fredericksburg.
WG: Of wounds rec'd at Gettysburg.
Co: Company

	KILLED.			WOUNDED.			DIED.			PRISONERS.		
	F	C	G	F	C	G	WF	WG	D	F	C	G
Field and Staff,	..	..	1	1	..	1	..	..	..	..	4	..
Co. A,	2	..	..	5	..	..	1	..	5	..	37	..
Co. B,	..	..	..	8	..	1	4	..	3	..	38	1
Co. C,	3	1	2	9	1	2	2	1	3	..	27	..
Co. D,	3	..	5	12	1	11	4	1	4	..	2	1
Co. E,	4	1	..	3	3	1	..	..	1	2	29	..
Co. F,	..	..	2	17	3	6	3	..	1	..	6	1
Co. G,	..	..	..	4	..	3	..	..	1	..	25	..
Co. H,	4	1	1	8	2	..	..	..	2	1	30	1
Co. I,	1	..	..	13	1	..	2	..	3	..	39	..
Co. K,	2	..	..	6	2	..	..	..	1	..	42	..
Total,	19	3	11	86	13	25	16	2	24	3	280	4

Killed and wounded at Fredericksburg,	105
Killed and wounded at Chancellorsville,	16
Killed and wounded at Gettysburg,	36
	—
Total killed and wounded,	157
Deaths in battle and by wounds at Fredericksburg,	35
Deaths in battle and by wounds at Chancellorsville,	3
Deaths in battle and by wounds at Gettysburg,	13
	—
Total deaths by battle,	51
Deaths by disease,	24
	—

Total deaths by battle and disease,	75
	—
Total killed, wounded, and deaths from disease,	181
Taken prisoners,	287
	—
Total casualties,	468

ARMY COMMANDERS OF THE TWENTY-SEVENTH.

Army of the Potomac.

Major-General Ambrose E. Burnside,

Major-General Joseph Hooker,

Major-General George G. Meade.

Right Grand Division.

Major-General Edwin V. Sumner.

Second Army Corps.

Major-General Darius N. Couch,

Major-General Winfield S. Hancock.

First Division.

Major-General Winfield S. Hancock,

Major-General John C. Caldwell.

Third Brigade.

Brigadier-General Samuel R. Zook.

Fourth Brigade.

Brigadier-General John R. Brooke.

FIELD AND STAFF.

Rank.	Name.	Residence.	Date of Commission.	Remarks.
Colonel,	[B]Richard S. Bostwick,	New-Haven,	Oct. 2d, 1862,	
Lieut.-Colonel,	[B]Henry C. Merwin,	New-Haven,	Oct. 2d, 1862,	Promoted from Captain, Co. A. Killed at Gettysburg, July 2d, 1863.
Major,	Theodore Byxbee,	Meriden,	Oct. 2d, 1862,	Resigned, March 28th, 1863.
Major,	[B]James H. Coburn,	New-Haven,	March 28th, 1863,	Promoted from Captain, Co. A.
Adjutant,	George F. Peterson,	New-Haven,	Oct. 6th, 1862,	
Quartermaster,	H. Lynde Harrison,	Branford,	Oct. 6th, 1862,	Resigned, Jan. 20th, 1863.
Quartermaster,	Ruel P. Cowles,	New-Haven,	April 1st, 1863,	Appointed from Captain, Co. H.
Chaplain,	John W. Leek,	New-Haven,	Nov. 10th, 1862,	Resigned, March 25th, 1863, by reason of wound received at Fredericksburg.
Surgeon,	Wm. O. McDonald,	New-York,	Jan. 17th, 1863,	Discharged for promotion, May 23d, 1863.
1st Asst.-Surg.,	Thomas M. Hills,	New-Haven,	Oct. 27th, 1862,	Discharged, Feb. 2d, 1863.
2d Asst.-Surg.,	Frederick S. Treadway,	New-Haven,	Oct. 18th, 1862,	Resigned, March 24th, 1863.

NON-COMMISSIONED STAFF.

Rank.	Name.	Residence.	Remarks.
Sergeant-Major,	Edmund B. Cross,	New-Haven,	Promoted 2d Lieutenant, Co. B, March 25th, 1863.
Sergeant-Major,	[B]Francis A. Foster,	Milford,	Appointed April 16th, 1863.
Q. M. Sergeant,	Charles A. Baldwin,	New-Haven,	Appointed Oct. 8th, 1862.
Com.-Sergeant,	John H. Steadman,	Meriden,	Appointed Oct. 8th, 1862.
Hospital Steward,	Jesse W. Henry,	Orange,	Appointed Oct. 8th, 1862.

[B] Taken prisoner at Chancellorsville.

OFFICERS OF THE LINE.

Rank.	Name.	Residence.	Date of Commission.	Remarks.
COMPANY A.				
Captain,	Henry C. Merwin,	New-Haven,	Sept. 8th, 1862,	Promoted to be Lieut.-Colonel, Oct. 2d, 1862. Killed at Gettysburg, July 2d, 1863.
1st Lieutenant,	James H. Coburn,	New-Haven,	Sept. 8th, 1862,	Promoted to be Captain, Oct. 2d, 1862, and Major, March 28th, 1863.
2d Lieutenant,	[B]Frank D. Sloat,	New-Haven,	Sept. 8th, 1862,	Promoted to be 1st Lieutenant, Oct. 2d,

				1862, and Captain, March 28th, 1863.
2d Lieutenant,	[B]Frank M. Chapman,	New-Haven,	Oct. 2d, 1862,	Promoted to be 1st Lieutenant, March 28th, 1863.
2d Lieutenant,	[B]Adelbert P. Munson,	New-Haven,	March 28th, 1863,	Promoted from 1st Sergeant.
COMPANY B.				
Captain,	Calvin L. Ely,	Branford,	Sept. 13th, 1862,	
1st Lieutenant,	Daniel W. Fields,	Wallingford,	Sept. 13th, 1862,	Resigned, March 25th, 1863.
2d Lieutenant,	[B]George W. Elton,	Wallingford,	Sept. 13th, 1862,	Promoted to be 1st Lieutenant, March 25th, 1863.
2d Lieutenant,	[B]Edmund B. Cross,	New-Haven,	March 25th, 1863,	Promoted from Sergeant-Major.
COMPANY C.				
Captain,	Addison C. Taylor,	New-Haven,	Sept. 11th, 1862,	Died, March 13th, 1863, from wounds received at Fredericksburg.
Captain,	[B]Ira S. Beers,	New-Haven,	March 13th, 1863,	Promoted from 1st Lieutenant, Co. G.
1st Lieutenant,	[B]Wm. R. Harmount,	New-Haven,	Sept. 11th, 1862,	
2d Lieutenant,	Chas. B. Brooks,	New-Haven,	Sept. 11th, 1862,	
COMPANY D.				
Captain,	Cornelius J. Dubois,	New-Haven,	Sept. 10th, 1862,	
1st Lieutenant,	Frank H. Smith,	New-Haven,	Sept. 10th, 1862,	
2d Lieutenant,	Ellsworth A. Smith,	New-Haven,	Sept. 10th, 1862,	Resigned, April 16th, 1863.
2d Lieutenant,	Sewell A. Dodge,	New-York,	May 17th, 1863,	Promoted from 1st Sergeant.

COMPANY E.				
Captain,	George F. Hotchkiss,	Woodbridge,	Sept. 13th, 1862,	Resigned, April 20th, 1863.
1st Lieutenant,	[B]David S. Thomas,	New-Haven,	Sept. 13th, 1862,	Promoted to be Captain, May 1st, 1863.
2d Lieutenant,	Wm. S. Rawson,	New-Haven,	Sept. 13th, 1862,	
COMPANY F.				
Captain,	Joseph R. Bradley,	East-Haven,	Sept. 9th, 1862,	
1st Lieutenant,	De Witt C. Sprague,	New-Haven,	Sept. 9th, 1862,	Honorably discharged, May 4th, 1863.
2d Lieutenant,	Charles P. Prince,	East-Haven,	Oct. 18th, 1862,	Promoted to be 1st Lieutenant, May 17th, 1863.
2d Lieutenant,	Daniel Worcester,	East-Haven,	May 17th, 1863,	Promoted from Sergeant.
COMPANY G.				
Captain,	Theodore Byxbee,	Meriden,	Sept. 3d, 1862,	Promoted to be Major, Oct. 2d, 1862; resigned March 28th 1863.
1st Lieutenant,	Ira S. Beers,	New-Haven,	Sept. 3d, 1862,	Promoted to be Captain, Co. C, March 13th, 1863.
1st Lieutenant,	[B]Stillman Rice,	Madison,	March 13th, 1863,	Promoted from 2d Lieutenant, Co. I.
2d Lieutenant,	[B]Samuel T. Birdsall,	New-Haven,	Sept. 3d, 1862,	Promoted to be Captain, Oct. 2d, 1862.
2d Lieutenant,	Frank B. Wright,	Meriden,	Oct. 3d, 1862,	
COMPANY H.				
Captain,	Ruel P. Cowles,	New-Haven,	Sept. 11th, 1862,	Resigned, April 1st, 1863, to accept Quartermastership.
1st Lieutenant,	Jedediah Chapman,	New-Haven,	Sept. 11th, 1862,	Promoted to be Captain, May 13th, 1863. Killed at

				Gettysburg, July 2d, 1863.
2d Lieutenant,	[B]Orrin C. Burdict,	New-Haven,	Sept. 11th, 1862,	Promoted to be 1st Lieutenant, May 13th, 1863.
2d Lieutenant,	[B]Winthrop D. Sheldon,	New-Haven,	May 13th, 1863,	Promoted from 1st Sergeant.
COMPANY I.				
Captain,	[B]Chas. M. Wilcox,	Madison,	Sept. 10th, 1862,	
1st Lieutenant,	[B]Samuel M. Smith,	New-Haven,	Sept. 10th, 1862,	
2d Lieutenant,	Stillman Rice,	Madison,	Sept. 10th, 1862,	Promoted to be 1st Lieut., Co. G, March 13th, 1863.
2d Lieutenant,	Charles W. Ely,	Madison,	March 13th, 1863,	Promoted from 1st Sergeant; resigned June 4th, 1863.
COMPANY K.				
Captain,	Bernard E. Schweizer,	New-Haven,	Sept. 10th, 1862,	Killed at Fredericksburg, Dec. 13th, 1862.
1st Lieutenant,	[B]Oswald Eschrich,	New-Haven,	Sept. 10th, 1862,	Promoted to be Captain, Feb. 28th, 1863.
2d Lieutenant,	[B]Christian Weller,	New-Haven,	Sept. 10th, 1862,	Promoted to be 1st Lieutenant, Feb. 28th, 1863.
2d Lieutenant,	[B]Wm. Muhlner,	New-Haven,	Feb. 28th, 1863,	Promoted from 1st Sergeant.

[B] Taken prisoner at Chancellorsville.

COLOR-BEARERS.

SERGEANTS.

James Brand.
Amos N. Benton.

By Promotion.

John F. Sanford.

COLOR-GUARD.

CORPORALS.

James L. Ambler.
John M. Bristol.
James W. Baird.
Joseph R. Clark.
Joseph B. De Witt.
John F. Sanford.
Sydney R. Thompson.
Henry E. Wing.

By Promotion.

William L. Bodwell.
Sydney H. Plumb.
Joseph Stevens.
George W. Tibbals.
George E. Treadwell.

PROMOTIONS AMONG THE ENLISTED MEN.

COMPANY A.

Third Sergeant Adelbert P. Munson to be First Sergeant and Second Lieutenant.

Corporal Henry C. Shelton to be First Sergeant.

Corporal George Ashdown to be Sergeant.

Privates William H. Cornwall,

Miles A. Goodrich,

Samuel J. Hilliard,

Sherwood S. Thompson,

Samuel L. Stevens, to be Corporals.

COMPANY B.

Privates Walter E. Fowler,

Henry W. Hubbard,

John K. Wilder, to be Corporals.

COMPANY C.

Corporal Charles S. Beatty to be Sergeant.

Private James Mulligan to be Corporal.

COMPANY D.

First Sergeant Sewell A. Dodge to be Second Lieutenant.

Fifth Sergeant George B. Lego to be Fourth Sergeant.

Corporal Fitch M. Parker to be Fifth Sergeant.

Augustus T. Freed to be Third Sergeant.

George T. Swank to be First Sergeant.

Private William E. Wilson to be Corporal.

COMPANY E.

Privates George Clemson,

Isaac Bradley, to be Corporals.

COMPANY F.

Second Sergeant Daniel Worcester to be Second Lieutenant.

Fifth Sergeant Stiles L. Beech to be Fourth Sergeant.

Corporal Thomas Ward to be Fifth Sergeant.

Private Moses Thomas to be Corporal.

COMPANY H.

Private Winthrop D. Sheldon to be First Sergeant and Second Lieutenant.

Private Origen Parker to be Sergeant.

Privates Amariah Bailey,

William A. Parmalee,

William G. Martin,

Edward McCormick,

Ambrose W. Hastings, to be Corporals.

COMPANY I.

First Sergeant Charles W. Ely to be Second Lieutenant.

Privates James R. Matthews,

John N. Watrous,

Henry Walton, to be Corporals.

COMPANY K.

First Sergeant William Muhlner to be Second Lieutenant.

Corporal Louis Trappe to be Sergeant.

Private Carl H. Hager to be Corporal.

PIONEER CORPS.

A.

Charles J. Morris.

B.

George W. Baldwin.
Nelson Vibbert.

C.

Sylvester R. Snow.

D.

Henry E. Smith.

E.

John B. Hartshorn.

F.

Elizur E. Page.

G.

Nelson N. Beecher.

H.

Edward E. Gamsby.
David Ford.

I.

Corporal Henry
  Walton.

K.

Adam Rutz.